FIONA CAPP

that oceanic feeling

ALLEN&UNWIN

First published in 2003

Allen & Unwin
83 Alexander Street
Crows Nest NSW 2065
Australia
Phone: (61 2) 8425 0100
Fax: (61 2) 9906 2218
Email: info@allenandunwin.com
Web: www.allenandunwin.com

National Library of Australia
Cataloguing-in-Publication entry:
Capp, Fiona.
That oceanic feeling.
Bibliography.
ISBN 1 74114 166 4.
1. Capp, Fiona. 2. Authors, Australian – 20th century – Biography.
3. Novelists, Australian – 20th century – Biography. 4. Journalists – Australia –
Biography. 5. Surfing – Australia – History. 6. Australia – Social life and customs.
I. Title.
A823.3

This project has been assisted by the Federal Government through
the Australia Council, its arts funding and advisory body.

Designed and typeset by Ruth Grüner
Maps and illustrations by Verity Prideaux
Printed in Australia by Griffin Press

To Leo

One line placed on the canvas committed her to innumerable risks, to frequent and irrevocable decisions. All that in idea seemed simple became in practice immediately complex, as the waves shape themselves symmetrically from the cliff top, but to the swimmer among them are divided by steep gulfs and foaming crests. Still the risk must be run; the mark made.

Virginia Woolf, TO THE LIGHTHOUSE

CONTENTS

FOREWORD

WHEN I STARTED the journey I am about to describe I imagined
I would end up telling a simple story about a woman approaching
forty with a young child, and a skeleton in the closet in the form of
a surfboard stashed away in the garage of her family's beach house.
A woman who gave up surfing in her early twenties, not long after
she got a job as a journalist in the big city, but who swore that she
would one day return to the water. I knew it would also be a literary
journey, about a love of the sea which is inseparable from a love of
books, as well as an intellectual one about why the 'idea of surfing'
has such a powerful hold over her imagination; in this sense, it
would be an attempt to marry the life of the body with the life of the
mind. I thought of this woman as someone with whom anyone might
identify; anyone, that is, who was familiar with the kind of discontent that comes of life in a postmodern city where the natural
world is confined to little plots of green space known as parks –
Freud called them 'reservoirs of fresh air' – or the even littler plots
of green space that are our gardens; the kind of discontent that comes
of driving in air-conditioned cars and working in air-conditioned
offices and cutting ourselves off from all that is elemental and

awesome and wild. This woman's journey back to the water, her rediscovery of that part of herself she had effectively packed away with her board, would also be a rediscovery of the coastline she had known and loved as a girl but had since become a stranger to.

She is, of course, me.

But the story quickly grew much than bigger me. As I ventured beyond this familiar coastline with all its clotted memories, beyond the borders of Australia, out into the immensity of the Pacific and eventually to Europe, I found myself a bit player in a story of epic dimensions: a story that goes back to a time when the Polynesians, those Vikings of the Pacific, first discovered that they could walk on water and dreamed up a cosmology in which the gods surf from island to island while lightning splits the sky. In this way, my story grew to encompass the story of these first surfers and their world, and the eventual collision of that world with Enlightenment Europe.

As I travelled in time and place, this ever-swelling story – like a wave which gathers energy as it travels across the ocean – acquired insight and inspiration from the stories of people I encountered along the way and of those who accompanied me for periods of the journey. Yet even as I travelled outward from the coast where it all began, this odyssey cast my heartland into sharp relief. Even as I began to understand why the 'idea of surfing' packs such an emotional punch, why it has become emblematic of individual freedom and humanity's yearning to be at one with the natural world, the sea on my doorstep was delivering up a very different story. This story was also about the quest for freedom but of a much more desperate, life-and-death kind. It was a story about refugees in flimsy boats risking everything on a voyage across an unknown ocean – an ocean which offers no solace or exhilaration or peace, only terror and uncertainty and the ever-looming prospect of death. For the two years I document here, their larger, more urgent story shadowed and haunted my own.

In Nevil Shute's apocalyptic 1957 novel *On the Beach*, Melbourne is the last place on earth untouched by nuclear war. The film adaptation starring Gregory Peck and Ava Gardner opens and closes with the image of an American submarine passing through the Rip at Port Phillip Heads like one of the last great dinosaurs of the sea. The submarine has fled to Melbourne because there is nowhere else in the world untouched by nuclear contamination. Popular myth has it that during the filming, Ava Gardner quipped that Melbourne was a perfect place to make a movie about the end of the world. In fact, the quip was the invention of a Melbourne journalist. Like many Australians, I was used to seeing Australia in this apocalyptic light, as somewhere stuck away at the bottom of the world; was used to making pilgrimages to Europe as though it was the centre of civilisation. Then I went to Europe with the eyes of a surfer for whom the Pacific is not a blue desert isolating us from the rest of civilisation or a vast moat protecting us from the northern hordes but the very hub of our watery planet. During this trip, I realised that in the two years since I had returned to the water, I had not only recovered a dormant part of myself. Something quite dramatic and unexpected had happened to my perception of the globe, to my assumption that ocean is an absence of land, and to my sense of where the centre and margins might lie. Tectonic plates had begun to shift in my mind and the world would never again look quite the same.

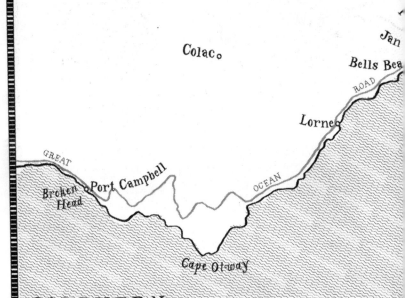

AUSTRALIA

VICTORIA

Ge

Jan

Bells Bea

Colac

Lorne

GREAT

Port Campbell

Broken
Head

OCEAN

ROAD

Cape Otway

SOUTHERN

OCEAN

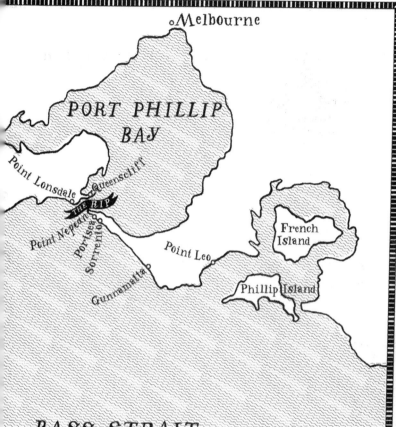

Melbourne

PORT PHILLIP
BAY

Point Lonsdale

Queenscliff

THE RIP

Point Nepean

Portsea

Sorrento

Gunnamatta

Point Leo

French
Island

Phillip Island

BASS STRAIT

Prologue

ONE LATE AFTERNOON in mid-winter, when I was three months pregnant, I took some visiting French friends to the Point Nepean National Park because they were keen to see the notorious entrance to Port Phillip Bay known as the Rip. The park was soon to close for the day so we quick-marched past the gun emplacements and the maze of underground bunkers at Fort Nepean and did not pause until the land fell into the sea. Around the corner, to the left, in Bass Strait, the surf was thunderous; line after line of ragged, blue barrels shattering into foam. To the right, Port Phillip Bay was shot silk with occasional white caps. Yet in this narrow strip of ocean between the Heads – this bottleneck where the bay and the strait collided – surfing conditions were perfect. I knew the Rip was a prized surf break but it still took me by surprise. At its worst, during a south-westerly gale on an ebb tide, the difference between the sea level inside and outside the bay could create a wall of water that broke from Head to Head. Today, a light south-easterly was blowing. Just inside the bay, to the right of the breaking waves, a small motor boat hovered;

I took it to be a fishing vessel until I saw a tiny figure paddling nearby.

I had spent many hours imagining my way into such a moment in my first novel, *Night Surfing*, but I had never seen it for myself. Although surfers have been coming by boat to this break they call Quarantine, Corsair, the Rip or the Point for decades, until twenty years ago it was regarded as a secret spot surfed only by the cognoscenti. On my previous visits, there had not been a surfer in sight. Now, absorbed by the figure of the surfer, I did not notice a giant ship stacked high with rusty red, orange and green containers approaching from Bass Strait. Suddenly its massive bulk loomed at the gateway of the Heads. The ship nosed steadily forward, dwarfing everything it passed. Soon after, another ship approached from the bay, this time in the south channel, much closer to the Corsair break. Against it, the surfer was a mere fly on an icypole stick. No wave would ever loom so precipitously or darkly above him, or cast such a shadow. For a brief moment, a trick of perspective put the surfer and the vessel on a collision course, before the ship slid calmly by, bequeathing him its wake.

Point Nepean was a forbidden place when I was young. Apart from the Bass Strait and Westernport coastline, it was the only wild bit of the Mornington Peninsula left. Until 1988 this area was an army officer cadet training school and closed to the public. I had only ever seen Point Nepean in the distance from the Sorrento–Queenscliff ferry: a rugged, tea-tree covered headland tapering away to a small, half-moon beach, with the remnants of an old fort and the colonial-style buildings of the former quarantine station just inside the bay. The minor incursions made by man on this tip of coast only accentuated its air of isolation. I was amazed there was a beach at all, that it hadn't been swept away by the powerful currents and surging tides of the Rip.

The other image I had of Point Nepean was taken from a postcard that was pinned to the back of the kitchen door at our Sorrento beach house. It was an aerial shot, a seagull's-eye view of this promontory carpeted in green and surrounded by the deep blue of Bass Strait looking as benign as frozen jelly. I would often study this postcard as if it showed some far-off land. In maps of the time, this end of the Peninsula appeared as an empty space. The rest of the region was a network of roads and built-up areas, but all roads stopped at the beginning of the army reserve. The road through the reserve wasn't even marked – as if its existence was a government secret that could not be divulged. What intrigued me most was that this narrow arm of land separated the wilds of Bass Strait from the dreamy waters of Port Phillip Bay. I had always thought of them as two distinct worlds. The bay I associated with childhood, with sand castles and lazy, endless afternoons spent snorkelling or floating on my back staring at the sky. When I was about ten years old, my older sisters and brother grew restless with this 'kids' playground' and we began to spend more time at the ocean beaches of Sorrento and Portsea, beaches which were to become the stage upon which my rites of passage to adulthood would be played out.

Sometimes we would go walking in a straggling line along the endless stretch of Portsea back beach to the crumbling arch of London Bridge. The walk always ended where the barbed-wire fence was strung across the cliff tops and signs told of unexploded shells, warning us to 'Keep Out'. Occasionally we would hear reports of gunfire as the officers in the army training camp practised on the rifle range. We knew that deep inside this territory there was a graveyard belonging to the old quarantine station, and an ocean beach where a prime minister had drowned, and a rocky stretch of coast upon which an untold number of ships had come to grief. It wasn't until I was in my late teens, when all prohibitions were a red rag, that I dared sneak into this forbidden zone. And it was much later still, after I had witnessed the lone surfer riding the tanker's wake, that I dared admit to myself that I too wanted to surf the Rip.

I knew it was a crazy idea. I hadn't surfed for fifteen years. Occasionally, when the subject of surfing came up in conversation, I would remark that I still had my wetsuit and board and that I intended, at some stage, to return to the water. But as I entered my late thirties, the claim was starting to sound wishful and even hollow; an expression of nostalgia rather than genuine intent. I lived in the inner suburbs of Melbourne, a hundred kilometres from the surf, and I now had a young child; life had settled into a comfortable routine. And yet, when sitting in the local park watching the other parents playing with their children, I would be gripped by a quiet feeling of panic. During holidays, as I swam in the shorebreak at Sorrento back beach and played with my baby boy in the rock pools, I would find myself casting furtive glances towards the surfers out beyond the break, like Prufrock watching the mermaids riding seaward on the waves and wondering, 'Do I dare?' If I didn't make a move to join them soon, I feared I never would.

I had always known that water was my element. When I was a girl, I wanted to be a swimming instructor. The man who taught me to swim had an indoor pool in his backyard and ran a private swimming school. The pool was less than twenty-five metres long, yet in my child's eyes it was vast. Gold veins of reflected sunlight danced on the ceiling, the air was fuggy with chlorine and voices echoed strangely as if in some undersea chamber. Pools were greener then. And like some ancient shepherd, the instructor would stand at the edge holding a long pole with a crook to rescue floundering children. I loved the other-worldliness of this steamy, glassed-in realm; this place where normal boundaries seemed to dissolve. But as I grew older and my family began spending more time at the ocean beaches, I discovered the slap-in-the-face exhilaration of the surf and the call of the blue yonder. The finite world of the swimming pool lost much of its appeal. In my restless, adolescent eyes it became an oversized concrete trench, the refuge of the landlocked suburbanite. There is no yonder in a swimming pool.

In my mid-twenties, I started work as a journalist and, soon after, gave up surfing. Although I learned to tolerate the hot, deserted streets of Melbourne in late December and early January when the rest of the world was 'down the beach', the young woman I had once been remained disdainful of the life I had chosen to lead, and I could never throw off the feeling that I was only half alive when I was away from the sea. Waves loomed in my dreams. I would be standing at the water's edge or perhaps bobbing in the shorebreak when, without warning, a mountain range would rear up out of the ocean and advance in slow motion toward the shore. I would feel the undertow, the suction of the oncoming waves dragging at my legs as I tried to scramble to the beach before the first wall of water descended. I'd wake before being engulfed but, strangely, I did not wake in fright. I was left, as always after dreaming about the sea, with a residue of hope and longing.

For many years I found a million good reasons why I couldn't take up surfing again. Then, one wintry day, when the novel that I had been wrestling with for months finally ground to a painful halt, I saw all my good reasons for what they were. A week later, I was in the car heading down to Sorrento to see if I could still squeeze into my old surfing skin, the wetsuit I had not worn for fifteen years. It hung on a hook in the corrugated-iron sleep-out behind our beach house along with all the old beach paraphernalia – buckets, beach balls, kick boards, boogie boards, hula hoops, deck chairs and badminton shuttles.

As I drove through the city and down the Nepean Highway lined with car yards and furniture showrooms, I thought of that moment when the Sorrento ocean beach road swoops like a gull diving, the tea-tree parting to reveal the etched blue lines of Bass Strait and the honey-combed amphitheatre of the back beach with its rock pools and heaving dumpers and seaweedy depths. I remembered how excited I had been when I took my French friends, Nelly and Marc, to the rotunda at the top of the cliff overlooking the beach. And how, as we gazed down on it all, I'd felt as proud as if I had carved those craggy, ochre cliffs myself; as if I had arranged for the waves to break in perfect, thunderous lines along the coastal shelf, leaving trails of milky lace; as if the flayed cheeks of the sand dunes and the wind-sculpted, rolling scrub and the silver coin of the bay behind us were my own creation. I wanted to tell Nelly, who speaks as little English as I speak French, what it meant to me. *C'est la côte de mon coeur*, I said, knowing it would sound corny in English, but hoping I could get away with it in French. *It is the coast of my heart.*

The suburbs of Melbourne seemed to go on forever; as if it was folly to try to escape them, as if this was the only kind of life you could lead. As I hit the Frankston freeway, which in my mind marks the beginning of the Peninsula, I slipped on a CD of the *Best of the Eagles*, the soundtrack to my surfing memories. The opening, twangy riff of 'Take It Easy' sent a shiver through my body and soon I was singing at the top of my voice, silently laughing at my nostalgia yet alive with a sense of adventure I had almost forgotten. The suburbs had turned into fields, the invisible ocean beckoned and I could hear the past rushing towards me with the explosive crackle of a broken wave.

In the 1940s, when my father was a boy, he spent his summer holidays camping amongst the tea-tree in the fore-shore dunes of the Sorrento back beach with his parents and a few other families. (Now the area is a national park and camping is prohibited.) They would play in the dumpers and swim in the rock pools and go fishing off a squat monolith called Darby's Rock, but to go out beyond the break was considered pure madness. They knew how quickly these beaches could become a graveyard for unwary swimmers. Occasionally they would catch sight of a tiny figure out the back where no other swimmer dared go, riding his giant, three-ply surf-ski. They knew him as Snowy Mann. He was the only surfer my father remembers seeing around these beaches when he was a boy and he cut a memorably heroic figure. Snowy's unwieldy ski made it hard work for him to get out beyond the break, and once there, he spent a lot of time paddling and positioning himself. But every wave he caught was a marvel. When he finally emerged from the water with the ski balanced precariously on his back, people would line the beach, clapping and cheering.

Things had changed dramatically by the time I began surfing in the early 1980s. Although no one looked twice at the sight of a black-clad figure sliding down the face of a wave, surfers were, in many respects, a race apart. Australia liked to promote itself as a surfing paradise, but surfers were a sub-culture still regarded with suspicion and bemusement by the mainstream. They were beach-bums, drop-outs, ragged-haired louts who spoke their own patois and, in my parents' eyes, could not be trusted with their youngest daughter. I had always loved the sea, and now I had fallen in love with a surfer and, through him, with the thrill of riding a wave. I was also in love with the spirit of rebellion that surfing embodied, the escape it offered me from my sensible, suburban self.

The *Best of the Eagles* was just finishing as I pulled into the driveway, cut the engine and ran straight to the sleep-out. I lifted the wetsuit off the hook, fully expecting it to fall apart in my hands. Gingerly I turned it out the right way, arm by arm, leg by leg, looking for spiders. A small one fell out and I pounced on it. A handful of sand gushed out and I wondered where it was from. The beach where I had last surfed: possibly Woolamai on Phillip Island, where I had reported on a surfing carnival. It hadn't been very satisfying: I don't think I caught a single decent wave. My surfing memories are littered with similarly frustrating experiences: surf too big or too small or too tricky for me to catch; getting stuck in the shorebreak and endlessly battling the white water; paddling out to the line-up only to be beaten to the waves by more experienced surfers; gutlessly pulling back from a wave I should have caught.

Above all, however, it was fear that had held me back in surfing and, later, kept me out of the water. Fear of failure, fear of being an impostor, fear of being out of control. (While the possibility of sharks always hovered at the back of my mind, it was a minor fear when surfing in Bass Strait.) All these fears coalesced in the tell-tale corrugations of a big set looming out the back, that unstoppable phalanx of pure, liquid energy from which there was no escape. It was my hope that this time I could begin to overcome the more debilitating aspects of this fear. And yet, perversely, the awe I felt in the presence of this natural force, a force so unfathomable that it grants you an inkling of infinity, was intrinsic to my attraction to surfing. The eighteenth-century philosopher Edmund Burke, and later the Romantic poets, called this phenomenon 'the sublime'. In Wordsworth's description of his younger self bounding over the mountains and the lonely streams of the Wye River valley 'more like a man / Flying from something that he dreads than one / Who sought the thing he loved', I saw myself out in the surf. The ocean was a source of the sublime, according to Burke, because it produced 'the strongest emotion which the mind is capable of feeling'. He emphasised the stimulating influence of the sublime on the imagination and so heralded a new, aesthetic relationship with the sea. 'I wantoned with thy breakers,' wrote Byron. 'They to me / Were a delight; and if the freshening sea / Made them a terror, 'twas a pleasing fear.'

Yet I knew that my love of the sea was not solely derived from the attraction of the sublime, the longing for awe. Most surfers – apart from those driven purely by the competitive urge – talk openly about the sheer joy of *being in the water* and the visceral need for an intimate relationship with the ocean. Informing this kind of understatement is a philosophy – sometimes couched in spiritual terms – about connecting with a force vastly greater than oneself, about returning to 'the source'. It harks back to a sensation invoked by the French writer Romain Rolland as 'the oceanic feeling'. Rolland used this metaphor when writing to Freud about an essay of the latter's that treats religion as an illusion. He agreed with Freud's views on religion but felt that he had not appreciated the true origin of religious sentiments. Such sentiments were born, Rolland wrote, of a feeling which was always with him and which others too had confirmed; a feeling which he described as a sensation of eternity; of something boundless or oceanic. Freud could not find this oceanic feeling in himself and did not regard it as the origin of religious belief. But he did concede that it may be a residual memory of that earliest phase of psychic life when the child and the world are one.

Few images better capture this primal 'at oneness' than that of the surfer crouched inside the crystal, womb-like tube of a breaking wave; an image made all the more exquisite by our knowledge of the wave's imminent destruction. No sooner has the surfer returned to that all-embracing amniotic realm than she is unceremoniously expelled into the harsh light of the world. In fact, this birth analogy is built into the Hawaiian word for surfing, *he'e nalu* – 'wave sliding'. *He'e* means 'to run as a liquid' or 'to flee through fear', while *nalu* refers to the surging motion of a wave or the slimy liquid on a newborn child.

Whenever I tried to pin down what this 'at oneness' felt like, one particular moment in the surf always came to mind. Whole years of my life have disappeared into a hazy blur but I have never forgotten these few seconds. I was surfing with a friend at one of the many breaks between Sorrento and Rye that can only be reached by hiking through the national park and clambering over acres of sand dunes. It was a glorious summer's day and it must have been very hot because I remember that I was wearing only a long-sleeved vest over a pair of bright red bathers. The swell was sizeable but not too big for me to handle. As soon as I began to paddle for the wave, I knew I had been waiting for it all my surfing life. I remember the water swelling beneath me and how I was perfectly in tune with its rhythm. I remember a surge of energy lifting me high above the hollowing water, the thickness of the shoulder, the glowing, desert-like appearance of the shore. Above all, I remember the instant at the top of the wave, just as I rose to my feet to 'take the drop', poised on the brink with the weight of the inrushing ocean behind me and the wave unfurling beneath me. The spool of my memories always froze at this last split second of clarity and separateness before the screaming descent where mind, body and wave became one.

Like one of Wordsworth's 'spots of time', it was a moment from the past that had remained preternaturally vivid, a singular memory that I could draw on for imaginative nourishment and solace during the course of daily life. The phrase 'spots of time' comes from Wordsworth's great poem 'The Prelude', but the idea is echoed in 'Lines Composed a Few Miles above Tintern Abbey', in which he speaks of the 'tranquil restoration' which his memories of the Wye River valley brought him when he was oppressed by the din of towns and cities. Wordsworth's version of the 'oceanic feeling', of the interconnectedness of all things, culminates in these famous lines:

And I have felt
A presence that disturbs me with the joy
Of elevated thoughts; a sense sublime
Of something far more deeply interfused,
Whose dwelling is the light of setting suns,
And the round ocean and the living air,
And the blue sky, and in the mind of man;
A motion and a spirit, that impels
All thinking things, all objects of all thought,
And rolls through all things.

In the lines that precede these, Wordsworth has been reflecting on how his relationship with nature has changed: how he has come to accept that the 'aching joys' and 'dizzy raptures' of his youthful encounters with nature are now a thing of the past. It is the perspective, you might think, of an old man. Yet at the time he was only twenty-eight years old – one year older than his sister Dorothy, whom he addresses in the second part of the poem. Dorothy reminds him of his former, untamed self. He assumes that she will, in time, take the same path as he did, that her 'wild ecstasies' will inevitably mature into 'sober pleasure', the pleasure of memory.

But was this path really inevitable? As I contemplated my return to the water, it wasn't sober pleasure I was after. Why couldn't the more mature understanding of nature as something we all 'half create' – through the meanings and desires we bring to it – co-exist with the immediacy of youthful rapture? I had to believe that it could. Otherwise I might as well sit back in my armchair and replay my surfing memories, and save myself the trouble of getting wet.

Cautiously I eased on the wetsuit. Apart from a tear at the base of the right leg, it remained in one piece. The cool, damp rubber over my body felt strangely familiar. I pulled up the zip and went to look at myself in the mirror. I grinned at my reflection. Fifteen years seemed to fall away. Flinging open the back door, I leapt down the steps and did cartwheels across the lawn.

The Idea of Surfing

SPRING

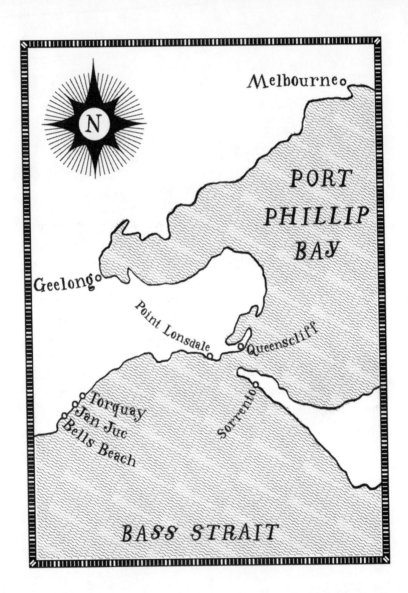

A MEASURED VOICE on the radio was forecasting storms as I drove west out of Melbourne. Beyond the flat, scrubby farming land on the city's outskirts, an ominous grey fuzz of low cloud blotted out the horizon. On the approach to Geelong, as the dark funnels and flame-lit chimneys of the Corio Bay oil refineries loomed in the distance, rain began lashing the car. If it hadn't been for an appointment I had to keep in Torquay, I would have turned around and driven straight home, mildly disappointed but secretly relieved that my return to the water had been delayed. Much as I wanted to surf again, I was afraid of what I would learn about myself. Ocean-lover James Hamilton-Paterson once wrote that he was almost as obsessed with the idea of the sea as with its actuality. I was afraid that when put to the test after all these years, I would be confronted with a similar but more unpalatable truth: that I was *more* in love with the idea of surfing than with the surfing itself.

The town of Torquay holds a special place in surfing lore because of its proximity to Bells Beach, one of the world's legendary surf breaks. But Bells is a hidden jewel reachable only through a bush reserve and a hike down a steepish gully. What hits you as you enter Torquay is the mercantile side of surfing in the form of a commercial estate on the highway into the town: a surreal 'village' of brightly coloured surf showrooms emblazoned with giant billboards of surfers on luridly blue waves. Two of the biggest surf companies in the world, Rip Curl and Quiksilver, began as cottage industries in Torquay in the late 1960s. Their presence, along with the Easter competition at Bells – the longest-running professional surf contest – has ensured that the town's identity is now inseparable from its surfing culture.

Those who knew Torquay in the 1950s remember it as a frontier town where a notorious group of wild boys associated with the Surf Lifesaving Club bought cheap land on the outskirts, whacked up some fibro shacks and called it Boot Hill. They were known for their heavy drinking, partying and love of pranks – one particularly memorable joke involved mowing the word 'Fuck' in giant letters into a crop of oats on a hill facing the town. Anyone who has not been to Torquay but has seen the 1991 American action film *Point Break*, in which the charismatic leader of a gang of Californian surfer-bankrobbers is finally tracked down to Bells Beach by the FBI, could be excused for thinking that Torquay is still a hillbilly, Wild West kind of town. In the final scenes, there is a shot of a sleepy main street with wide verandahs and a whistlestop train station with a sign announcing, 'Torquay (Bells Beach)'. It's all very quaint and countrified, like something out of *Northern*

Exposure, and it's nothing like Torquay. The real giveaway, for Australians at least, is the foreshore backdrop of firs and the grey shale on Bells Beach. Not a tea-tree or ochre cliff-face in sight. The film was shot, in fact, off the coast of Oregon in the USA.

I hadn't been to Torquay for at least six years, and as I drove past the surf showrooms, I felt a pang of nostalgia for the mythical Torquay of *Point Break* that would forever remain unsullied by the forces of big business. Yet even before the construction of the surf plaza and nearby Ocean View housing estate, the real Torquay – a modest mix of suburban brick veneers, fibro holiday houses, neat weatherboards and brash townhouses, with a shopping strip reminiscent of a suburban mall – had never borne much resemblance to its film counterpart. I was on my way to meet local surfer Grayme Galbraith, known as Gally, who grew up in Bell Street, Torquay. The street was named after the Bell family, who owned much of the local land, including the farm which gave Bells Beach its name. When Gally was a boy, the town was a haven for hippies, surfers and people wanting to escape the rat race. Living two minutes' walk from the beach, he spent much of his childhood in the water, but didn't take up surfing until he was eighteen. He now lived in the Ocean View estate, which had consumed the rolling farmland where that giant 'Fuck' had once been emblazoned. He only had to lift his head off his pillow in the mornings to inspect the surf through his bedroom window. Gally had been an Australian champion twice and state champion too many times to mention. Apart from selling surfboards for Rip Curl, he coached the state surfing squad and gave private lessons. Hence our rendezvous.

I no longer had friends who surfed and I did not welcome the prospect of surfing alone (not a wise thing to do when you're seriously out of practice), so I had asked Gally to give me some lessons. I had deliberately chosen the protected break of Torquay to save myself the kind of pounding I had endured when learning to surf in the unforgiving beach breaks of the Mornington Peninsula. Back then, it never occurred to me to ask someone to teach me: I didn't believe that surfing could be taught. Like writing, it seemed too fluid, too unpredictable an activity; too much a matter of individual talent and temperament. You had to work your way out from the shorebreak, get used to being dumped and spat out; you had to watch more experienced surfers and figure out what to do for yourself. In other words, you had to do it the hard way. Twenty years later, the hard way had lost much of its appeal. Apart from wanting company and advice, somewhere in the back of my mind was the memory of my swimming instructor with his long shepherd's staff ready to haul me clear of the water when I got into trouble.

At Torquay Point, the swell rolled around the headland and peeled off into neat, smallish waves ideal for novices. Intermittently, the sun broke through the pewter clouds making the cliff glow like a freshly baked loaf of bread. It was a weekday, and as I gazed out over Bass Strait contemplating the surf, I had a sneaking feeling that I was breaking some unwritten rule about how one should conduct one's life; that I ought be at my office in the inner city or at home looking after my young son. The storm that had brushed me on my way down was now unleashing a flash flood on Melbourne, having by-passed Torquay like a travelling show hellbent on making an impression in the big smoke. If I had paid more attention to the weather map and the wind direction I might not have written off the surf so hastily, but I was out of touch with reading those signs and contemplating what was going on in the ocean. A hot northerly wind could still have me hallucinating glassy waves, but my grasp of pressure systems and their impact on the swell had always been rudimentary. What I did know was that the winter months were the best time along the Victorian coast for powerful groundswells produced by lows in the Southern Ocean. The past May had been classic: nonstop six-foot waves and off-shore winds. Now it was September and the equinoctial winds had begun to blow. As always in the spring, the weather was unsettled and unsettling.

'Just what you want,' Gally announced, casting an expert eye over the water. It is no longer *de rigueur* for surfers to have the dishevelled, sun-bleached look, but with his shock of sandy hair almost to his shoulders, freckled tan, laconic manner and playful grin, Gally was unmistakably a surfer. He pointed out the various breaks between Point Danger at the far end of the beach and Torquay Point right in front of us at the creek mouth. The rip that travels out next to the rocky headland – a boon to the surfer but a hazard to swimmers – is known as the Escalator. 'We'll stay in the shorebreak for a while, then go out the back a bit further.'

After changing into my brand-new wetsuit – the old one was too thin for comfort in 14 degree water – I locked up the car. I was wondering what to do with my keys when I remembered a dream I'd had the week before. I was standing in front of the Doges' Palace in Venice looking out across the lagoon towards the white dome of Santa Maria della Salute when I noticed some figures on surfboards in the grey, choppy water. There were no waves, just the wake of vaporetti and tiny peaks whipped up by the wind. Some people, I thought, will do anything for a surf. Then, without warning, a perfect, glassy wave, began rising slowly out of the lagoon like a rare, exotic beast and I knew I had to get out there. As it happened, there was a nearby kiosk where I could hire a board. I pulled on my wetsuit and was preparing to enter the water when I became concerned about what to do with my keys and wallet. Should I bury them in the pebbles of the small beach in front of St Mark's Square? Surely they would get stolen. I spent so much time worrying about what to do with them that I woke up before I had a chance to put a toe in the water.

Feeling a little foolish, I asked Gally what he did with his keys.

He slammed the hatch of his station wagon and picked up his board. 'Hide them somewhere on the beach or under the car.' He was once so eager to get in the water, he said, that he left the keys in the ignition and the doors unlocked.

Still anxious about abandoning my keys, I rolled them in my towel, picked up the training board Gally had brought for me and headed for the beach. The symbolism of the dream was obvious enough. The keys represented my secure, predictable life; the life I was throwing open to risk and uncertainty by returning to the water.

I did not notice the cold at first. I was too bent on navigating my way through the white water that snapped at my heels like a pack of hungry terriers. When I was deep enough into the breaking waves, I turned to face the shore and started to paddle. A foaming wave picked up my board, sending it skidding forward as I seized the sides and scrambled to my knees before rising clumsily to my feet. In my late teens and early twenties, I would have been mortified to be seen mucking about in the shorebreak. Real surfers caught unbroken waves. Desperate to prove myself to the world, I took to paddling out the back with the experienced surfers before I knew what I was doing, and not infrequently found myself in situations that I did not have the skills to handle. I have no doubt that this made me more fearful than I would otherwise have been. While I was lucky not to have any truly hair-raising experiences, was never dumped so badly that I lost my nerve, I spent a lot of time avoiding waves when I should have been trying to catch them. If I had settled for smaller breaks closer to shore, I suspect my surfing memories would not be so fraught with ambivalence.

Two things had changed. First, I was older and didn't care about looking foolish or being uncool, didn't feel compelled to show that I could mix it with the boys. Here I was, on this great big spongy plank of a training board – the kind of thing I would never have been seen dead on twenty years ago – happy to take things slowly, to get it right. And second, surfing was no longer the distinctive, tribal subculture it had once been. When I was younger I was acutely conscious of the exclusiveness of the surfing scene and of its hostility to newcomers, especially women. Now that surfing had been absorbed into mainstream culture and lost its anti-establishment edginess, this 'them' and 'us' mood had largely evaporated. Ironically, while that shift made surfing easier for me now, I did not want to forsake what it had represented to me as a young woman – its sense of rebellion, its defiant existentialism, its rejection of the routines of mainstream life, its celebration of the uncontrollable power of the sea. For all the folly of revisiting the romantic dreams of my youth, here, in the water, I knew that the essence of surfing had not changed. The steps might have become more flashy but the dance on the wave remained the same.

With each successive wave, I was able to get to my feet more smoothly, catching nice little re-forming waves that appeared out of the white water like a staircase materialising from nothing. My stance, Gally warned, was too squat, feet too far apart; I'd never be able to manoeuvre the board if I didn't stand tall. It was time, he said, to go out a bit further, beyond the break. I paddled out, pushing against an invisible membrane of resistance. If anything, the years out of the water had sharpened and augmented my fear, not dulled it. When I was a child I loved being dumped and churned and flung about like a rag doll, loved being at the mercy of the wave. As an adult I seemed to have lost the art of abandon, of giving myself up to the ocean. I had my life so tightly under rein that I had forgotten the mad joy of letting go.

A little peak was looming. 'This one,' Gally yelled, and gave my board a shove to help launch me onto the wave. The nose of my board plummeted and the shoulder of the wave felt too steep, but somehow I got to my feet and quickly slid down the green face, then rode the broken wave all the way to the shore. After catching a few more like it, I was so awash with adrenalin I could barely think straight. All I could do was smile. Why on earth had I waited fifteen years?

During a brief lull between sets, Gally told me that I didn't need lessons every week. He said I should go out myself for a few weeks and then come back and see him so that he could correct any bad habits I'd picked up. I tried to hide my dismay as I told him that I didn't feel ready, that I needed the lessons to build up my confidence, that I had a problem with fear.

'It's only water,' he grinned. 'If you want to surf, you have to pay the rent.' Which was the very lesson he couldn't teach me.

After an hour in the water my feet and lips were numb. Back in the carpark getting changed, I asked Gally if he had surfed Corsair. I told him that I had written a novel about a young man who surfed there at night.

'Hah!' he laughed, brushing the sand from his feet. 'That would be the end of him.' Gally had surfed the Rip a few times but didn't bother any more because it had become too crowded. It was a great left-hander, he admitted, but very tricky.

At the time, I didn't dare tell him that it was my dream

to surf Corsair. A writer wanting to emulate one of her more reckless characters could easily come across as harebrained: I could imagine the look on his face. But a few weeks later, as Gally and I grabbed a coffee and muffin at a local cafe after my lesson, I decided to make my confession; it was time to find out whether I was kidding myself about surfing Corsair.

Whatever his feelings, he disguised them well enough. 'It would give you a fright,' he said, after a pause. He described how the powerful Bass Strait swell came driving through the narrow Heads and wrapped around Point Nepean, executing a sudden right turn. One moment the swell looked as if it was passing you by, the next moment the wave was coming right at you, hollow and fast. 'To be honest, I don't think you could handle it.'

What else could I have expected? The week before I had found the Torquay shorebreak on a biggish day a challenge. When I was dumped by an unexpected wave and the broken water held me down for a fraction longer than usual, I began to panic. Scrabbling for the surface, I gulped breathlessly through the foam before the wave was ready to let me go. Yet I was only under the water a matter of seconds. Gally had paddled swiftly over. You have to remember, he said, that you can hold your breath for at least a minute and that you'll never be held down for that long. The trick was not to fight the wave. By fighting it you only made things worse.

In the cafe, a small brown wave of coffee slopped over the side of my cup as I pushed it aside. 'I don't mean now!' I said, mortified. 'What about in a year's time?'

He gave the slightest of shrugs: he didn't want to commit himself to something so unpredictable. The whole idea must have struck him as a little mad. Here I was, a raw recruit fearful of three-foot waves at Torquay Point, dreaming of surfing Corsair.

The next two months were almost unrelentingly grey and rainy, and everyone I knew seemed to have grown sad, as if the low, dark skies had become a state of mind. We all hunkered down, waiting for the miserable weather to pass. Occasionally, I wondered if the uncertain pleasure of an hour in the water – it was too cold to stay out any longer – was worth the three-hour drive.

It wasn't just the weather that was grim and disheartening. The mood of the country – as far as one could judge from the media – was turning chillier by the month as alarm grew about the number of refugees, mostly from Afghanistan and Iraq, arriving by boat on the northern coast of Australia and outlying islands and reefs. A telling sign of the changing times were the epithets now used by the government to describe them: 'illegal immigrants' and 'queue jumpers'. There was, I thought, a certain dignity about the term 'boat people', which had been coined to describe the refugees who came to Australia in boats from Vietnam and Cambodia two decades ago. It reminded us of the dangerous odyssey that the refugees had made, linking them with the successive waves of people who had travelled to Australia in boats from the First Fleet onwards. It placed them within the long tradition of nomads of the water driven by necessity to abandon their homeland and take enormous risks in order to find a safer place to live. The government's new labels only served to turn the boat people into criminals and to harden our hearts against them.

Like the ploughman in Brueghel's *Icarus*, one grew used to going about one's life while absorbing news of misery and disaster from near and far. But as I drove down to the surf with the radio issuing regular reports on the fate of the boat people, I could not but be aware of the vast gulf between my relationship with the ocean and theirs; the gulf between what I was free to do, and what was happening to them in their small, often unseaworthy vessels on the seas between Indonesia and northern Australia, or locked up in bleak detention camps on the edge of the Australian desert. I had always regarded going down to the sea as a kind of secular baptism. But now I could not look at the ocean horizon, which was traversed by all manner of ships and small craft, without being conscious that the view had changed. The ocean, that vast symbol of physical and spiritual liberation, that locus of epic adventure, had taken on a much darker aspect. For the boat people, the sea was not a playground but a giant moat and a death trap. Amid the static and chatter of communication between vessels on the sea for business or pleasure, other voices were now carried on the wind. Like most Australians I could choose not to hear those voices. But the sea is like the unconscious: it tosses up scraps of debris and *memento mori* when we least expect it. The repressed inevitably returns.

For many years I'd believed that I couldn't take up surfing again if I didn't have a companion; it seemed too daunting on my own. And yet now, in a matter of weeks, my lessons with Gally had given me the confidence to make the weekly trip alone. While I loved the sense of adventure that came with hitting the road and leaving the city behind, especially on a weekday when everyone else was heading for work, my mood was always tempered by anxiety. What if the conditions were no good? Of course I had studied the weather map and the surf reports. But forecasts were not infallible and there was no substitute for being able to see the waves for yourself. Things could change unexpectedly: the wind might turn on-shore or the swell might suddenly drop away. I would constantly check the windsocks and lines of bunting I passed along the way, watching for signs of change. If I saw surfboards on cars heading back to the city, I fretted about why they were leaving the surf behind. There was also the guilt that came from leaving my twenty-month-old son at childcare while I took off to the surf. If I had not been surfing, I would have been working and he would still be in crèche, so what difference did it make? Now that I'd begun writing this book, surfing and work had become inseparable: I was writing about surfing and surfing to write. But I could hardly expect anyone who saw me dropping off my son at the crèche with my surfboard strapped to the car roof to believe that I was 'going to work'.

Once I was in the water, these anxieties fell away. The

rough and tumble of the ocean did its work. By the time it came to the drive back home, I was scoured clean like a shell, inside and out. I reeked of the sea. Crystals of salt clung to my eyebrows and my head was wonderfully empty of the fretful static that it had played host to on the way down. I had done what I needed to do. Now I could return to the city and, for a while, I could be content.

One afternoon I wandered into the Surfworld Museum at the back of Torquay Plaza, my hair still wet and matted from surfing, my head in a dreamy daze. 'Come and discover', the brochures promised, 'why everyone is a surfer deep inside'. For all its slickness, I liked the way this catchline captured the atavistic allure of the activity, the seductive power of the idea of surfing, even for those who would never dream of surfing themselves.

The first exhibit in the museum and the first image of surfing made by Europeans was a copy of a watercolour by John Webber, the official artist on Captain James Cook's third voyage to the Pacific, titled 'A View of Kealakekua Bay'. It depicts Cook's triumphant yet peaceful arrival on the island of Hawaii in January 1779. Double and single canoes full of Hawaiians crowd the water around the ships *Resolution* and *Discovery*. In the middle foreground a small figure is paddling a surfboard over the choppy water towards the ships; near the shore, another figure is pushing a surfboard out through waves. Stone cliffs rise above a sweeping, crescent-shaped bay. In the south-eastern corner is a coconut grove, a beach, some huts and a temple.

Webber's drawing does not, however, capture the full, chaotic drama of the welcome the Hawaiians gave Cook in the belief that he was an incarnation of Lono, their great god of the land. In his journal, Lieutenant James King speaks of fifteen hundred canoes and at least three hundred women and young boys swimming from the shore to the ships, as well as 'a number of men upon pieces of Plank'. In a series of remarkable coincidences, Cook had arrived at the time of the Makahiki festival, of which Lono was the patron. Over this four-month period of freedom and celebration, the common people were released from the rule of the chiefs. Taboos could be broken with impunity, gender roles were reversed. There was much feasting and great tournaments of many kinds including boxing, sledding, running, javelin-throwing and surfing. A procession of priests around the island to mark Lono's return ended at the temple on the beach where Cook first landed.

While surfing had been practised throughout the Pacific for thousands of years, in Hawaii it reached an unrivalled level of sophistication. The songs and *meles* or chants through which Hawaiian history and traditions were transmitted were full of stories about surfing romances, surfing gods, great surfing exploits and other surf-related dramas. Surfing was inseparable from the religious, sexual and social rituals of traditional Hawaiian life. My knowledge of this history was sketchy when I first set eyes on that copy of Webber's painting. But I sensed how big the story of surfing was; how surfing as a sport and as an emblem of ancient Polynesian society was caught up in one of the most significant moments in world history, the moment when Enlightenment Europe stumbled on what it believed to be an earthly 'paradise' – only to destroy it. One of the great catch-cries of the Enlightenment, epitomised by the French Revolution, was 'freedom'. Freedom from arbitrary power, freedom of speech, freedom of trade, freedom to make one's way in the world, freedom from want, freedom from superstition and fear. In the first European impressions of surfing, we find a perfect symbol of this longed-for freedom. A symbol which, despite surfing's increasing commercialisation, still has currency.

Beneath the Webber print in the Surfworld Museum is a brief quotation about surfing from Cook's journal, in which he remarks that being 'driven on so fast and so smoothly by the sea' must be a 'most supreme pleasure'. It comes from an entry made when the explorer was in Tahiti during his third voyage. One day, when Cook was walking at Matavai Point where he and his men were camped, a man in a canoe on the sea below caught his eye. The islander was looking about with an eagerness that Cook found suspicious: he thought the man must have stolen something from one of the ships and was being pursued. Then he realised that the islander was, in fact, absorbed in catching waves, and was totally uninterested in the Europeans' ships and tents close by.

He went out far from the shore, till he was near
the place where the swell begins to take rise;
and, watching its first motion very attentively,
paddled before it, with great quickness, till he found
that it overtook him, and had acquired sufficient
force to carry his canoe before it, without passing
underneath. He then sat motionless and was carried
along, at the same swift rate as the wave, till it landed
him upon the beach. I could not help concluding
that this man felt the most supreme pleasure while
he was driven on so fast and so smoothly by the sea,
especially as, though the tents and ships were so near,
he did not seem in the least to envy or even to take
any notice of the crowds of his countrymen collected
to view them as objects which were rare and curious.

Like Cook's observation that the soothing effects of this motion seem, as music can, to allay 'perturbation of the mind', the episode reveals his extraordinary appreciation of surfing's power to enthral the surfer's whole being to the exclusion of all else. The Tahitian surfer's world is soon to be turned upside down by contact with the West, yet he is neither beguiled nor distracted by the trappings of European civilisation. At this particular moment, he is a picture of self-contained serenity – surfing is all that matters.

When Cook's journal and Webber's sketches were first published in Europe in 1784, they created a sensation. Here were Jean-Jacques Rousseau's 'noble savages'. Here was a southern Arcadia: the utopia that Europeans had thought existed only in their imaginations, an ideal society free of hypocrisy, toil and sexual inhibition. Here was an 'ocean of desire' – as Bernard Smith puts it in *Imagining the Pacific* – in which all the nations of Europe would come to wallow. Yet it was on this third voyage that Cook became painfully aware that his grand role as Enlightenment Man was riven with contradictions, writes Smith. 'Cook increasingly realised that wherever he went he was spreading the curses much more liberally than the benefits of European civilisation.' Hence his obsession with being portrayed by Webber as the great Pacific peacemaker. To modern eyes, though, Webber's painting of Cook's arrival in Hawaii looks more ominous than triumphant. Hindsight has given it the appearance of Eden at the moment of the Fall, with surfing providing a nostalgic emblem of man living in perfect harmony with nature; a harmony about to be shattered by the forces of civilisation.

In *Civilisation and its Discontents*, Freud turns this argument on its head when he blames the 'voyages of discovery' for much of the Western world's discontent with civilisation. These voyages, he says, encouraged the mistaken belief that native peoples were 'leading a simple, happy life with few wants, a life such as was unattainable by their visitors with their superior civilisation'. For Freud, humanity's struggle for happiness is a tug of war between the desire for individual freedom – which springs from that part of ourselves untamed by civilisation – and the necessarily restrictive demands of society. In Freud's history of civilisation, there is no period in which man cosily cohabits with nature, no lost idyll. Nature is man's greatest adversary, a force to be feared or tamed. Civilisation – as symbolised by great European cities such as Rome – has been driven by the struggle for self-preservation in the face of nature's 'crushingly superior' forces. In *The Future of an Illusion*, he writes of how the elements 'seem to mock all human efforts to control their lives: the earth, which quakes and is torn apart and buries all human life and its works; water which deluges and drowns everything in a turmoil; storms, which blow everything before them.' Civilisation is humankind's bulwark, paid for by the renunciation of our most basic instincts.

What Freud doesn't address – but what explorers like Cook did seem to intuit – is how the repressed element of our psyches might find *release* in these potentially threatening forces of nature, just as they do in sex. That was how I had always understood surfing. And yet my dream of a perfect wave looming up out of the murky waters of the Venice lagoon seemed to endorse Freud's logic. Few symbols of Western civilisation better embody its fragility and artifice, its ongoing struggle for mastery over the natural world, than does Venice. A wave such as I had imagined would spell the destruction of this fairytale city built upon a collection of swampy islands and forever threatened by the encroaching sea. If this dream was any indication, my unconscious fear was that I could have only one or the other: Venice or the wave.

Everyone, in their own way, spends their life negotiating ways to ameliorate the discontent of which Freud writes. For many years, the act of writing had provided me with a deeply satisfying means of giving vent to unconscious or repressed desires and urges. But my recent novel had faltered, I suspected, because my life had become too rarefied and inward-looking, too circumscribed; too removed from nature and from the world outside my window; too 'civilised'. I had to get out of my head and surfing provided the way.

Jack Finlay's loungeroom jutted into a garden of well-tended greenery like the helm of a ship nosing through a sunlit, turquoise sea. On the mantelpiece above a large stone fireplace sat sea-worn marble doorknobs, fragments of crystal decanter stoppers and glass tumblers, an ink bottle still full of ink, a bronze timber fastening and other small relics Jack had collected from wrecks over the years. At one end of the mantelpiece, next to a stuffed pheasant, was a selection of Jack's most treasured sea books: Conrad's *Typhoon* and *The Mirror of the Sea*, Stevenson's *In the South Seas* and *Island Nights Entertainments*, and Cousteau's *The Silent World* stood alongside works on early Polynesian navigation and voyages of exploration.

Jack was sitting in a straight-backed armchair near the fireplace, his hands making emphatic little jabs in the air as he talked. Every now and then he would leap out of the chair to find a book or video and urge me to take it home. For the past two months we had been meeting after my surfing lessons, talking about surfing and sizing each other up. Jack had been one of Gally's high school teachers. When I told Gally we'd met, he asked if I'd noticed Jack's stance. He planted his feet slightly apart, standing springy on his toes: 'He used to be a boxer.' I knew that Jack surfed, sailed, dived but not that he had boxed. I thought of the way his hands moved as he spoke, the way he hunched slightly forward, his eyes fixed on yours as if daring you to strike first; his air of contained energy and emotion. That summer, when watching Jack surf, I would see the boxer again, in the steadiness with which he rose to his feet, planted himself on the board and stayed there. He wasn't much interested in fancy manoeuvres, but the comet-like way he streaked across the wave was timeless.

Jack had cropped white hair and pale, freckled skin. There was something about his penetrating gaze, his alertness and habit of firing back questions that gave him the air of a genial cop. He had taught in high schools, worked for the CSIRO and spent seven years running the Surfworld Museum at Torquay (the Webber print was the first exhibit he installed). He had written stories and books about surfing and sailing, and was now writing a book about the uncertain fate of the ageing boxer.

Since returning to surfing 'midway life's journey', I had been shamelessly searching for my own Virgil to guide me through the many circles of the surfing world, an insider who was not so far inside the culture that he couldn't see its faults. I knew nothing about Jack when I plucked his slim volume of stories, *Caught Inside*, from the shelves of the La Trobe Library. Most books about surfing are either 'how to' or travel guides, histories of the sport, biographies of legendary surfers or analyses of surfing as a subculture. But Jack's book was different. It was unashamedly literary. The lead story in the collection, 'Fat City', was about a disillusioned surfer and his friend, an Aboriginal boxer called Jacky Paradise, who upstages a surfing competition by releasing a bag of snakes on the beach. It was a beautifully wrought fable, and at the same time, a subtle, ironic commentary on surfing mythology, the price of joining the mainstream and what surfing has lost in the process. The subtitle, 'The life and times of a surfing legend', didn't refer to any of the competitors. The legend was Jacky Paradise with his bag of snakes.

The story reminded me of a conversation I'd had with Gally about the forthcoming state finals at Bells, in which he was competing in the masters' division. I asked him if the division after 'masters' was 'veterans'.

'They don't call them that any more,' Gally said. 'They're legends.'

We both laughed at the pomposity of it. And what came after 'legends'? Gally snorted, 'The grave.'

In his author's note to *Caught Inside*, Jack said that he wrote out of a love of surfing and a conviction that there was more to surfing than surfing. When I read that I knew I'd found the ally I had been looking for. I rang him and told him what I was doing. 'Come around and we'll talk,' Jack said. And so one day after my lesson, I called in at Jack's Torquay home and our conversations began.

Right from the start it was evident that our lives and approaches to surfing were very different. Jack grew up by the bay and, except for a short stint teaching in Gippsland, had always lived a life devoted to the sea, away from the big cities. He had little time for those he saw as 'inner city wankers' who spent their days at cafes in bohemian Brunswick Street. The world of 'learned doubt' and 'chattering apes', which, as A. D. Hope puts it, 'is called civilisation', held little interest for him. That I worked in a room above a pub near Brunswick Street and could be found, on any given day, eating my lunch at one of its many cafes, didn't change Jack's mind: he could see that I was torn between that world and his, whereas he knew where he wanted to be. I envied him his certainty. The Peninsula might be my heart's coast but I doubted that I could live there.

But much as he was happy in Torquay, it was a surf company town and Jack was not exactly a company man. He appreciated the jobs the industry brought and respected the skills that kept it running, but was critical of what he regarded as the aridity of surf culture, its narcissism and its obsession with youth. He believed that the surf industry and media, in their constant pursuit of a 'cool' image, were largely to blame. This idea of 'cool', he believed, was a form of commercially motivated elitism, a marketing concept that only detracted from the freedom of surfing.

Gradually, I learned that just as I felt like an outsider in the surfing world, Jack felt himself an outsider in what he perceived as *my* community, the literary world. That sense of alienation united us. And above all, we shared a fundamental understanding that outweighed all our differences: an understanding of the powerful hold that surfing can have on the imagination, how it can become a metaphor for life, how it can haunt your dreams.

Jack came to surfing as a young man in the mid-1950s during holidays spent in Sorrento. His family owned the house that had been the original school in the early days of the town's settlement. When he was a boy, Jack's father would take him out in a fishing boat trolling for yellow tail in the Rip. They would see gigantic swells rolling down the side of the rusting wreck of the freighter, the *Time*, marooned on the rocks near Corsair. Their little boat would be bobbing like a piece of flotsam and Jack would invariably be sick. Sometimes a large wave would surge towards them, and as his father swung the wheel to bring the boat around, Jack would see agitation in his movements. He grew up thinking of the Rip as a fearsome place.

In 1959, Jack's father bought him a purple and black sixteen-foot plywood surfboard known as a 'toothpick' because of its narrowness and pointy ends. His father didn't know that a revolution had taken place in surfing with the introduction of the shorter malibu boards from California in 1956, and that the toothpick was out of date. When compared with a malibu, it was long and unwieldy; a potentially dangerous missile to anyone swimming or surfing nearby – not to mention Jack himself. One day his sister was on the beach at Portsea when she heard some people who were watching the surf cry out. She looked up to see her brother's purple and black board shooting high in the air before crashing down on Jack's head just as it emerged from the water.

In the early years of his marriage, when Jack and his wife,

Sue, were living on a yacht in North Queensland, he met an American sailor who had come to Australia after the Battle of the Coral Sea. The sailor had a peacock and a pig tattooed on his foot. It was an old sailors' superstition that if you had a bird tattooed on your foot, you wouldn't drown. So Jack got a bluebird tattooed on his foot and for many years it seemed to serve him well. Then, one Anzac Day in the late 1970s, he pushed his luck. A big swell was running at Bells, the waves between eight and ten feet. Jack was looking after his son Carl. Knowing he could trust the five-year-old to stay put, he marked out an area on the beach where the child could play and where Jack could see him from the water.

It was hard going from the start. Because of the size and strength of the swell it took Jack three attempts to get out through the breaking waves. He was so drained by the time he reached the line-up that he tired quickly, and after less than an hour he decided to head in. He was paddling for the impact zone – where the waves rear up and begin to break – in order to catch a wave to shore, when he heard a sharp yell from surfers further out. A huge set was approaching and he was in a bad position. He managed to scramble over the first wave and was furiously paddling up the towering face of the second, when, realising that he might not make it, he jumped off his board and shoved it through the crest of the wave. The crest broke over him and dragged him down, and when he came up out of the foam he could feel his leg rope stretching as the wave dragged his board away from him. He gulped some air before being wrenched down again into the turbulence, but the strain was too much for his leg rope. It snapped, leaving him adrift without his board. There was nothing to do but swim.

Jack could see his son still playing on the beach. He knew he had to get into shore before the current running up the coast carried him towards the rocks at Winkipop, but he was already exhausted. For the first time in his life, the prospect of drowning had become terrifyingly real. Without his board he was much more vulnerable to the relentless barrage of explosive white water. He managed to body surf towards the shore, taking a pounding as he went. Soon he was tantalisingly close to the beach but couldn't break free from the undertow. One moment he would be dumped onto the sand, then just as he was beginning to claw his way up the steeply sloping beach, another wave would sweep his feet from under him. Time and again he scrambled from the water only to be dragged back down into the boiling shorebreak. By now there was no strength left in his arms and his legs had turned to jelly. He had almost given up but managed to summon the energy for one last dash. This time, he was able to scramble free of the wave before it sucked him back, and to drag himself up the beach. Utterly spent, he fell on his knees, his chest heaving. When he was able to move, he scooped up his board, which had washed ashore nearby, and staggered back towards the small figure of his son, who was still playing happily on the sand.

Towards early November, there were signs that the gloomy weather was lifting. Fat-bellied dragonflies could be seen darting over the foreshore dunes. Bass Strait was growing warmer, the wind less chilling. In my dreams, giant waves didn't just rear up out of the ocean, they collapsed right on top of me like the mouth of a whale slamming shut. As the water came crashing down, I would tell myself that there was nothing to fear because I would soon wake up. And strangely enough, when I returned to the surf I managed to invoke that calm. Then I bought myself a new surfboard – a seven-foot-four 'hybrid' – and with that simple act of commitment, everything began to change.

My twenty-two-month-old son stood with his nose pressed to the wire door watching me as I strapped the new board in its shiny, silver cover to the roof of the car. When I had first brought the new surfboard home, his eyes had turned into saucers. Now he had taken up a chant which I could hear from the footpath.

'Wow! Mama board, Mama board, wow!'

He had quickly discovered that the board was kept under the 'big bed' and he would often visit the bedroom to check on it. When we were at Sorrento one weekend, I found an old orange kickboard that I had used as a child out in the bungalow and gave it to him. 'My board!' he cried, thoroughly delighted. Pointing to the car where the mama board was strapped to the roof, he indicated that he wanted his put there too.

Like all children of his age, the boy was becoming

increasingly wilful and determined to have his way. 'My' had become one of his favourite words. He was leaving behind that early stage of development in which the world was an extension of himself, moving beyond that phase of limitless narcissism which Freud regards as the origin of the 'oceanic feeling'. As I heard myself saying 'No' to him a thousand times a day, it seemed ironic that I was required to oversee the civilising process of my son at the very time I was bent on giving expression to the 'untamed' element of my psyche through surfing. If he was to become a stable and happy human being able to take his part in society, teaching him to master his basic instincts was something that I, like all parents, had to do. It was not a role I enjoyed and it often felt like a vigil without end. I took comfort in the rapturous way he responded to the beach and the ocean and the mysterious forces that moved the water. I did not want him to lose touch with that anarchic, untamed part of himself; if I was to be honest, I did not want him to lose touch with that earliest phase of his existence which connected him most intimately to me. I told myself that when he was old enough, I would teach him to surf.

As it happened, the day I baptised my new board at Jan Juc – just around the corner from Torquay – there were a number of kids in the water being given lessons by their fathers. Jan Juc was a beach break, a long stretch of sand similar to Portsea on the Peninsula except that the surf tends to be smaller and a little gentler, the rips much less treacherous. I had my new 'grown-up board' and I felt a bit like a kid myself with Gally in the role of surrogate father. I watched one of the surfers launching his two spiky-haired young sons onto some of the smaller waves, envious of the ease with which these nine- and ten-year-old boys angled themselves on the wave, making the most of the unbroken face in a way that I was yet to master. Amongst those of us vying for the waves was another older novice, and in his hesitation and awkwardness, I recognised myself. I noticed how he hung back from the critical take-off point of the wave and how he tried to catch the waves from the shoulder, often missing out because he was never quite in the right spot. And I understood all too well why he wasn't: to position yourself in the ideal spot to catch a wave can feel akin to placing yourself in the path of an oncoming express train. Your natural inclination is to get out of the way.

'C'mon, get out here!' It was the father calling out to his sons, who appeared more interested in mucking about in the shorebreak than in paddling out for another wave. As I was leaving the water, the boys were grabbing handfuls of tea-coloured foam and flinging it at each other.

Back in the carpark, Gally ran into a friend of his whose nine-year-old daughter had also been out in the surf.

'I wish I'd started when I was nine,' I said to her father.

'Don't we all,' he replied.

And perhaps that was the truth of it: the old story of parents urging their children to the heights they wished they'd reached when they were young.

The irony of wanting to teach my son to surf was that I myself would probably never have taken it up if my parents had urged me to – which they didn't, although they gave me and my siblings every chance to enjoy the surf when we were young and we spent blissful hours on our surf mats at Portsea during summer. In fact, when I first took up surfboard riding, the activity was so intertwined with a host of self-conscious acts of rebellion, defiance and angst-ridden love that it was rarely as much fun as it had been when I was a girl.

In late spring, during a period when the swell was small, I finally felt ready to return to the Peninsula. The day was sunny and warm when I left Melbourne, and I was looking forward to my first chance to surf under a blue sky after so many months of grey. But by the time I had left my son with my parents at Sorrento front beach, the wind was turning south-easterly and I was certain the surf at Portsea would be a mess. The road to the back beach climbs up over the foreshore dunes, and as you descend to the carpark, the ocean opens out like a deep blue fan. If the surf is good you can see the lines of swell approaching from far out in the ocean. And when the surf is big, it can look as if the horizon has broken its moorings and is advancing towards the shore. The cliffs above the beach are so high that a chairlift – now defunct – was installed in the 1960s to ferry people between the carparks and the beach. From this vantage point, I gazed out over the long stretch of beach, from the natural arch of London Bridge shrouded in seaspray at one end to the rocky outcrop of the Sphinx at the other; beyond it, I could see the biscuity, wind-blasted cliffs that stretched to Cape Schanck, twenty-five kilometres away. So unimpeded was the view that the earth's curve registered in the horizon.

In recent years when I had come to Portsea, I had confined myself to that liminal, shifting zone where water and land meet. Much as I loved this beach, I found it hard to be completely happy here now that I no longer surfed. I was always conscious that something was missing. I would go walking along the sand and swimming in the shorebreak but I never ventured far out. Over the years, I had poured all my energy into becoming a writer, and had allowed my horizons to shrink. Now it was as if a door had been flung open inside me, a door to a vast and wonderful room to which I had denied myself entry.

As always, most of the long beach was empty except for the stretch of sand in front of the clubhouse, which was thick with people. To my surprise, the surf was not a mess after all: it was a little choppy, but I knew immediately that these were conditions I could handle. I took the wooden steps down the cliff with my board under my arm, remembering how excruciating I used to find this grand entrance: the painful visibility of being a lone woman with a board. There was something about Portsea's reputation as the haunt of 'the beautiful people' – or perhaps it was just because I was young – that had always made me feel I was stepping onto a stage here. This time, the glances meant nothing to me. I waxed my board and headed for the water. The sandbank in front of the clubhouse was still there, with rips to the left and right of it. Instead of suffering the old indignity of being pounded by the shorebreak, I slipped easily into the left-hand rip, which carried me swiftly out the back. I exchanged nods with the two other surfers out there, and we all got on with making the best of the choppy conditions. There was nothing special about the waves I caught that day, but what made it memorable was the simple act of being out there again and feeling at ease; of putting my fears into perspective. I had not realised that a body of water could have such distinctive contours, that it could feel so familiar after so many years. It was as if I had come home.

An hour later, I was paddling back to shore when I saw a man in his twenties bobbing in the water nearby, calling out to his friend on a surf-ski, who was too far away to hear. He had the build of a strong swimmer but the rip seemed to have caught him off guard and he was floundering. He looked across at me, his face a mixture of embarrassment and alarm. 'Could I hold on to your board for a bit?' he asked. 'The cold's taken me by surprise.'

I paddled over and he grabbed the back of my board. 'You're in a rip,' I said, wondering if he realised; so many people didn't. The surf-lifesaving movement had placed billboards along the main routes to the coast with the message 'Avoid the R.I.P.' The problem was that most people didn't have the ocean awareness to recognise a rip, let alone avoid it. 'Here comes a wave, we'll catch this one in,' I said.

When we reached a depth where he could stand up, the

man let go. 'Thanks,' he said. 'I'll buy you a drink at the pub some time.' Then he headed for the shore.

A few weeks later I went out again at Portsea feeling almost cocky, only to be reminded how changeable, almost manic, the topography of the water could be. The surf was solid and unforgiving, the shorebreak at its dumping best. It was folly, of course, to believe that you could ever be at 'home' at this beach. There would be days when I would roll up at Portsea to find it close to primeval. From out of a soupy haze, gigantic humps of water like an army of kraken bent on self-destruction would be rolling shoreward before beaching themselves, the water covered with a vast white skin of broken capillaries from the backwash of the waves. Sometimes the haze would be so thick that the ocean would seem to have just emerged from the mists of time, as if it had never been surfed and never would be.

Entranced by that mythical line where sea meets sky, Tennyson's Ulysses regarded all experience as 'an arch where-through gleams that untravelled world whose margin fades for ever and for ever when I move'. I once saw that archway in a dream. It loomed up out of the water at Portsea, like the famous Torii gateway in the sea off Miyajima Island in Japan, except that my dream arch was an imposing Roman structure made of stone. I was just about to go to Europe for six months. In the dream, I knew that Europe and all the promise of life yet to be lived lay on the other side of that portal. What did it matter that Portsea faces the Antarctic?

Surfers were forever hovering on the verge of departure, of launching into the unknown. All that horizon-gazing while waiting for waves gave life a particular orientation. If I had an image of the future, it was of an ocean horizon – the fine thread upon which all our hopes hang. In certain conditions when you were out surfing, clouds massing along the horizon or the quality of light could make islands appear in the distance. Atlantis beckoned. What stopped the inquisitive surfer from paddling out in pursuit of these chimera was the endless promise of perfection embodied in the approaching waves. Your destination came to you, each wave with its own story of distant lands.

One 35 degree day at Jan Juc, I was gazing out to sea when I noticed something strange happening on the horizon, a trick of light bouncing between sky and sea. It was low tide and the water was a translucent turquoise. White cabbage butterflies and other small insects were darting over the waves.

'Take a look at the horizon,' I said to a surfer with whom I had fallen into conversation. I had never seen anything like it but did not want to mention what it looked like for fear of sounding melodramatic.

'Looks like a tidal wave, doesn't it?' he replied.

Exactly what I was thinking: it looked as if a giant wave was steaming towards us in a great wall of foam.

Most of our waves in southern Australia are generated by cyclones in the high latitudes of the Indian and Southern oceans close to Antarctica. Coasts in the southern hemisphere are, as Rachel Carson so hauntingly put it, 'washed by waves that have come from lonely, unvisited parts of the ocean, seldom crossed by vessels, off the normal routes of the air lines'. Even a surfer in California can find herself riding waves born in the west-wind belt of the screaming Sixties that circle Antarctica. Oceanographers can spot the signature of these Southern Ocean waves in their frequency, rapidity and the direction from which they come.

Our waves come from the deep south but our cultural ties bind us to the north. My abiding sense that Europe lay on the other side of the horizon had always complicated my feelings about surfing. When younger, I felt that my two touchstones – surfing culture and European culture – belonged to two separate, incompatible universes. Modern surfing, as opposed to the ancient Hawaiian art, was a New World, not an Old World, phenomenon. Although surfing was now popular in France, Spain, England and other parts of Europe – I once saw a surfer in the Baltic Sea – it was the *idea* of surfing that helped me close the gap between my two spheres. I had written my first novel in the belief that surfing could symbolise something much larger than the act itself – that it could transcend culture and place. But it was not until *Night Surfing* was published in France and Britain that I knew with certainty that surfing as a metaphor for life could indeed resonate as powerfully for someone in Paris or London as it could for an Australian.

I was talking to Jack about all this one day, when his eyes lit up at the phrase the 'idea of surfing'. He showed me a book of wave photography to which he had contributed the text. His essay described a surfing epiphany he had experienced during a trip to Florence in 1996. He was manager of the Surfworld Museum at the time and had been asked to assist with the production of surfing graphics and film footage to complement a surfwear pavilion at an Italian trade fashion show. He had always longed to visit Europe and now, at fifty-two, his chance had come, courtesy of surfing. So great was his joy at finally finding himself there that he would wake in the early hours of the morning in his hotel bed in Florence and find himself laughing out loud.

Jack was brought up a Catholic but after a year spent in a boarding school run by the Sisters of Mercy where beatings and screamed abuse were part of the daily routine, he learned to regard the church with deep wariness. His gradual rejection of Catholicism, however, did not mean the end of his spiritual quest. Soon after his arrival in Florence, he wandered jet-lagged into the Basilica of Santa Croce, a Franciscan church dating from the second half of the thirteenth century. The iconography of his childhood, he was surprised to find, was still deep within him. 'Surrounded by 600 year old frescoes and the tombs of Renaissance figures such as Michelangelo and Machiavelli,' he later wrote, 'I found myself in a small alcove to the lower left of the main altar. A cluster of candles burned before a statue of the Virgin. Who had lit each one of these, I wondered, and for what hopes did those flames flicker? From the corner of my right eye a movement caused me to half turn. There, in the gloom and grey of the vault that reached above the main altar, a single shaft of light had hit the gold embossed crucifix suspended perhaps four metres above the ground. In that instant, for the first time in my life, I understood with great clarity the basis of my own religious impulse, its relationship to the great sweep of human endeavour, and my long and fruitless search for peace, with its metaphor of the perfect wave.'

Later, he writes about sitting on a stone wall outside Fiesole, talking with some friends about surfing. 'It was Giannino who used the term "the *idea* of surfing" in describing how the activity itself blurred at the edges and became something far bigger, into which all people could reach for whatever it was they sought . . . In the upper reaches of the Arno Valley, somewhere out there in the night, a perfect wave stood up, feathered, then peeled off flawlessly along the edges of my mind.'

Summer was approaching and the water was growing warmer and more inviting. Mid-sentence, I would find myself looking up from my computer to gaze out of my office window at the large eucalypt in the garden across the road or, more precisely, at the movement of the wind through its slender leaves. One glance and I could tell if a northerly or a southerly was blowing. If the wind was northerly, there would be good waves somewhere within a two-hour drive of Melbourne. I would start to feel restless, my concentration disturbed by an irritable hankering for deep blue lines of swell rising to meet the sky. Like a self-imposed exile or a desperate lover entangled in an illicit affair, I knew I was not where I wanted to be.

Somehow, I had to learn to live with the tension that came of being pulled in opposite directions; with the constant shuttling between two different ways of life. In *Civilisation and its Discontents* Freud reminds us that happiness can only ever be episodic. 'When any situation that is desired by the pleasure principle is prolonged, it only produces a feeling of mild contentment. We are so made that we can derive intense enjoyment only from a contrast and very little from the state of things.' I was putting the best face on my frustration with not being able to surf at will. And yet surely it was true that much of the pleasure I derived from surfing was heightened by the fact that it was an episodic, mercurial and intermittent experience. Over a year later, I would meet a French surfer, a self-proclaimed 'spotologist' – a specialist in surf spots – whose research showed that most surfers could tolerate only so much perfection. After just four days of ideal surfing conditions, ennui set in and perfection began to pall.

I often wondered whether I would be any happier if I lived by the sea. As Jack and I argued about the relative merits of each way of life, I began to suspect that I would always be torn between the two. In her small classic, *Gift from the Sea*, the American writer Anne Morrow Lindbergh writes of her struggle for a balance between worldly, domestic demands and the need for solitude by the ocean; the endless cycle of retreat and return. The lesson we all have to learn, Lindbergh believes, is how to live with intermittency. 'How can one learn to live through the ebb-tides of one's existence? How can one learn to take the trough of the wave?' She invokes the image of a pendulum swinging between two poles. The two worlds, she seems to be saying, do not have to be brought together; they can co-exist and complement each other.

I longed for it to be so.

In late November, I told Jack that I had gone back to the Peninsula and surfed on my own. I described how it felt to return to Portsea and the confidence it had given me, and how I had decided to stop taking lessons from Gally. We talked, too, about what people meant when they spoke about the 'frontier of surfing', which had become something of a buzz term in the surfing press to describe surfing adventures to atolls in the Pacific or other remote destinations that had never been surfed.

'That's the conventional portrayal of the frontier of surfing,' Jack said. 'But there are also frontiers of surfing for someone who is never going to travel like that. Florence to me was a frontier of surfing. You might find your frontier of surfing at the Corsair break, or in the journey that's taking you there.'

At the same time, Jack was concerned that I had elevated Corsair into an almost mythical place which I would always believe was beyond my ability. The Rip held a special place in the popular imagination because of the many shipwrecks it had claimed, its strong currents, whirlpools and powerful, dangerous tides. But from a surfer's perspective, Jack said, it was not very different from some other surf breaks. For instance, in terms of its speed and hollowness, the wave at Corsair was similar to Beacon at 13th Beach on Victoria's southern west coast. He advised me to surf those waves, and also suggested going to Point Nepean at low tide and walking out on the rocks so that I could get as close as possible to the Corsair break. That way I could study it, make it familiar. Demystify it.

Then, with a sudden air of ceremony, Jack told me he had something for me. He strode across to the fireplace and from among the fragments of old glass decanters, door knobs from sunken vessels and other *objets trouvés* on the mantelpiece, he took three metal bullets which he had found at the firing range on Point Nepean.

Jack hadn't seen me surf yet, but he had a teacher's instincts. He knew that half the battle was believing that your goals were within your grasp, and that sometimes, other people's belief in what you were doing could make a difference.

'You'll do it,' he said, placing the bullets in the palm of my hand, as if they were talismans. 'You'll surf Corsair.'

CHAPTER 2

That Larger Playground

SUMMER

Then, suddenly, you see it, a blue hill going up and up, beyond the borders of the world, to the salt colored sky, and white whirling necklaces of gulls, and if you look long enough, a great vague ship solemnly going somewhere. I can't express how it makes me feel to see it again, there is a feeling of the most utter relief, as if I could close my eyes, knowing that I had found again someone who loved me years and years ago.

William Faulkner in a letter to his mother.

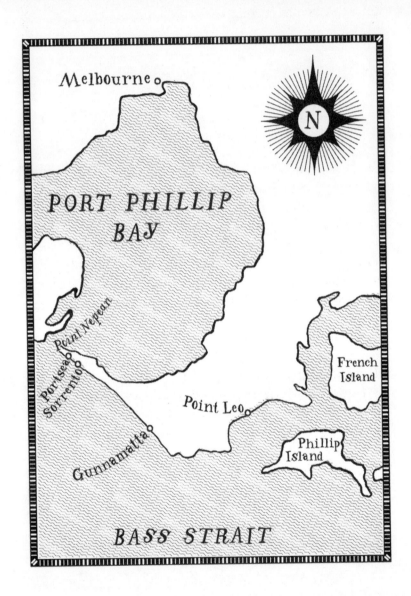

AROUND EIGHT O'CLOCK in the morning, as I left the family beach house at Sorrento for nearby Portsea back beach, the traffic was starting to build. As if some apocalyptic, meteorological beast was slouching towards us, the weather bureau had been issuing warnings for almost a week about the approach of a 40 degree day. Now that it had arrived, half of Melbourne was fleeing for the coast. Within hours, the Nepean Highway would be jammed with a shimmering ribbon of cars heading south.

I arrived at Portsea back beach to find an off-shore wind sculpting some clean peaks from a gentle swell under low, dark skies. A promising scene, except that a surfing contest was monopolising the best waves, which meant that the rest of us had to share one break. A surfer with any sense would lie low during the summer season, when it is permanently peak hour in the surf and when the swell is invariably small. But this year, I was not a surfer with sense. I was a surfer besotted. Much as I hated the summer crowds, I couldn't stay away.

As soon as I reached the line-up, I wondered what I was

doing there. The swell had dropped and the occasional wave rolled lethargically by as if it didn't have the energy to break. A large school of surfers circled hungrily. No one was overtly aggressive, but the frustration was palpable as three malibu-board riders and a surf-skier picked off the waves out the back before anyone else had a chance to get near them.

I was contemplating paddling straight back to the shore when I noticed a face that I hadn't seen in almost twenty years. I kept an eye on him as I jostled for position, not entirely sure whether it really *was* him. He too, I noticed, was looking inquiringly at me. I knew that I couldn't leave the water until we had spoken. For a while we both hovered amid the pack, paddling half-heartedly while the clouds shimmered in the water like lurking sharks. Eventually, I edged closer and caught his eye. Lori broke into a grin and we exchanged greetings, marvelling at how long it had been. Sitting on our boards, we measured the years with talk of our children and the struggle to find time to surf when you live away from the coast. I told him how I had recently returned to surfing; he said he hadn't surfed for a year; and we both roundly cursed the long-board riders who were hogging the waves. We didn't speak about the past but it lay beneath our conversation like the water beneath our boards. It was difficult to keep the talk flowing with one eye fixed on the surf and, just as we did all those years ago, we eventually drifted off in different directions in pursuit of those phantom waves. After a few futile attempts at catching one, I decided to go in. Why, I wondered, was I so reluctant to talk to Lori about the past or about the other surfers we both knew?

Why didn't I ask him about Mark? But Mark was a Peninsula local and Lori was a student from the city. They had never been close friends and had probably lost contact long ago. I kept paddling towards the beach, telling myself that it was best to leave the past and the turmoil of first love alone.

One morning in early December when I was seventeen years old, I stepped onto the familiar scaly sand of Sorrento back beach with a surfboard under my arm, conscious that something momentous was about to happen. The sky was faultlessly blue, the sea tinged with green. Mark was already in the water. I crouched at the sea's edge fumbling with my leg rope, watching him paddle out. I loved the lean, graceful shape he made on the board whether he was sitting or paddling or standing on a wave; the casual finesse with which he would execute a 360° turn before flicking out of the wave at the end of the ride. No matter how many surfers were in the water, I could always pick his lithe, electric figure from the pack.

We had met the year before. He was the only local amongst a group of engineering students from the city who hung out at Sorrento back beach. He had left school after Year 11 and was working for the national parks. I had grown up with a head full of poems about the sea, and in this archetypal surfer with tangled blond hair, searing blue eyes and wicked smile, I thought I had found the marine lover I was looking for. We were immediately drawn to each other, but it was an attraction of opposites; we were much too different to ever make it work and, inevitably, the relationship faltered almost as soon as it began. That summer, as it all fell apart, I watched Mark longingly, hating the distance and the silence between us, hating the horrible helplessness that left me stranded on the shore. It was then, as I rambled the cliff tops overlooking the breakers at Sorrento and Portsea, that I became determined I would learn to surf. All through my final year at school I ached to be by the sea, and whenever I got the chance, I would head down to Sorrento back beach and hold my breath as the water came into view, hoping to catch a glimpse of Mark's familiar figure on the waves.

The following summer, Mark and I met up again and I told him that I wanted to surf. As if he realised this was the only thing he could give me, he arranged for a friend to lend me a kneeboard and a wetsuit, and we drove in awkward, solemn silence to Sorrento back beach. I wanted to believe that this was a new beginning, a sign of what we had in common – our passion for the sea – but it was really Mark's way of saying goodbye, of launching me on my own. I watched him disappear into the waves and lumbered into the shorebreak after him, the board heavy under my arm, the wetsuit on back to front. Like all beginners I was clumsy and graceless, but as I scraped to my knees on the broken waves I knew beyond any doubt that I was finally where I wanted to be. Never again, I promised myself, would I sit on the beach feeling marooned and helpless, aching for what I couldn't have while real life unfolded out on the glittering sea.

As one of the few sheltered surf breaks along the Bass Strait side of the Peninsula, Sorrento back beach has been a nursery – of the school of hard knocks variety – to generations of surfers. Even last century, long before anyone dreamed of riding its waves, people flocked there to witness the spectacle of the surf and partake in 'a thorough rough-and-tumble and exhilarating ocean plunge'. As I played out my adolescent drama on this beach, drenched in the ecstatic pantheism of Coleridge and Wordsworth, and the melancholy music of Tennyson, I was experiencing my own version of the sublime as surely as those nineteenth century visitors to Sorrento, who savoured the intense emotions stirred by this 'noble' coastline. The author of the *Cyclopedia of Victoria* excitedly described the waves at the back beach as a pack of wild animals 'making frantic efforts to clamber up the rocky wall, roaring as they leap and then falling back again baffled and raging . . . '; while a wood engraving in *The Australian Sketcher* titled *The Back Beach of Sorrento: A Storm Outside*, clearly inspired by early Romantic artists like Caspar David Friedrich and J. M. W. Turner, depicts two windswept figures standing on a rocky outcrop during a storm, watching a sailing boat being lashed by the waves.

As it happened, the day I met Mark, I was sitting on a rocky outcrop at the back beach with the waves crashing at my feet, gazing out to sea. I had recently read John Fowles's novel *The French Lieutenant's Woman*, in which the mysterious and tragic figure of Sarah Woodruff, ostracised by Victorian society, is often seen standing at the end of Lyme Regis pier.

She is observed by the scientifically-minded gentleman Charles Smithson who, when he first sees her face, is struck by the candour of her gaze. 'There was no artifice there, no hypocrisy, no hysteria, no mask; and above all, no sign of madness. The madness was in the empty sea, the empty horizon, the lack of reason for such sorrow.' As I sat on my rock fancying myself as that solitary, enigmatic heroine, Mark was in the carpark watching me through a pair of binoculars. And like the French lieutenant's woman, I was aware of being observed and relished my role.

Shaped like an intimate, natural amphitheatre, the back beach invites and feeds this kind of imagining, as the theatrical entrepreneur George Coppin recognised. Coppin established the Ocean Amphitheatre Company in the 1870s and oversaw the building of a tramline to the back beach, a rotunda lookout at the top of the cliff, a 'coffee palace' over-looking the water, and foreshore paths of limestone with seats and shelters at convenient intervals. The paths remain, the rotunda and kiosk have been rebuilt, and the theatrical mood endures. To arrive here, no matter what the season, is to sense that you have entered an enhanced natural arena where something special and momentous is unfolding. It is to become a witness to – and possibly a participant in – a mysterious, endless performance upon which the curtain never falls.

Coppin and the other early founders of Sorrento were inspired by fashionable English curative resorts like Ramsgate and Brighton. Visitors could step off the steamer from Melbourne at the front beach pier, wander past the foreshore bandstand and outdoor baths, hop on the steam tram and be transported down the wide main street with its verandahs and attractive limestone buildings to be deposited at the back beach where they could witness the wild spectacle it offered, all with a limited amount of exertion or danger. If Romantics like Turner and Wordsworth showed man confronted by nature's chaotic and awesome violence, the Victorian impulse, as expressed here, was to employ the props of civilisation to make this violence picturesque; to turn nature into a sideshow.

Almost every room in our family beach house featured sepia photographs of old Sorrento: men in boater hats and women in high-necked blouses and ankle-length skirts disembarking from one of the steamers at the pier; a vista of the back beach at the turn of the century; the open-sided tram trundling past the Continental Hotel; elegant women with parasols promenading on the front beach. While the tram is now gone, the town has been well preserved, and this Victorian vision of Sorrento has remained the proscenium arch through which the ocean at this end of the Peninsula continues to be viewed. As wild as it is, its romance does not come from being remote, from being at the 'last edge', as Tim Winton describes the West Australian coast. When you sit on the cliff top to gaze out over Bass Strait, you are always conscious that civilisation is at your back, tastefully hidden among the tea-tree. Since childhood, my experience of the ocean had been mediated by these civilising props, by this late nineteenth-century impulse to partake of nature yet keep it safe. The ocean I knew was what Jonathan Raban calls the

Byronic brand of Romantic sea, 'in which every swimmer could wallow in the boundless, endless, and sublime and still be home in time for tea and muffins'. The legacy was hard to throw off and I was not entirely sure that I wanted to.

The year after my first surf at Sorrento, I bought a second-hand board but rarely had the chance to use it as I had no car to get to the beach. Because I had always spent holidays at Sorrento, it did not occur to me that I might be better off trying to learn to surf somewhere else. I didn't know that the ideal place to start was Point Leo, a protected series of reef breaks facing Westernport Bay. If the Peninsula is pictured as a pointy-toed boot with Point Nepean at its tip, Point Leo is somewhere around the lower calf. This is where most Peninsula surfers go during the autumn and winter months, when the waves are often too big for the exposed, Bass Strait beach breaks from Gunnamatta to Portsea.

Although increasing numbers of women were surfing further north, very few women surfed on the Peninsula in the early 1980s, and I rarely encountered those who did. As a self-conscious, reserved young woman for whom surfing and poetry were inseparable, I regarded myself as an outsider. My high-brow unease about the brash, Boys' Own, youthful swagger of surfing culture trapped me in chronic ambivalence and uncertainty about where I might fit in.

Much later, when I met some of the women who had surfed

on the Peninsula and west coast in the 1970s and early 1980s and asked them about how they had coped with the over-whelmingly male culture of the time, they talked of the necessity of being 'one of the boys'. I envied them as I knew that was not a role I could have played. The main difference between those women and myself, though, was not simply their ability to get along with their male peers, but the nature of their commitment and talent. The women who stayed in there for the long haul at that time tended not to be recreational surfers. They were driven. Surfing was their life.

Jan Dunton was one of them. The first summer of my return to surfing, I saw her at Point Leo. I was jostling for my own little scrap of sea among the two dozen surfers out, when a strongly built woman on a malibu board came stroking confidently toward the line-up. It was obvious from the breezy, muscular way she moved, smiling broadly and trading remarks with every second surfer she passed, that she was in her element. The surf was absurdly crowded but Jan slipped into the waves as if there were no one else around, walking the board and threading easily between the novices who lacked the dexterity to manoeuvre themselves out of the way.

When I visited her at home in the bushy, bayside town of Mount Martha, she told me that she had started catching waves on a foam kickboard at four years old. By the time she was in her teens, she was surfing for up to six hours a day with the local surfers at Point Lonsdale. Afterwards, they would all go to the pub and review the day's surf. In her early forties, after having had two children, Jan won the Australian malibu titles at Bells Beach. Even when her two sons were very young, she knew that she had to find an hour or two each day to spend in the surf. She was living at Point Lonsdale then, a minute's walk from the Rip. All Jan had to do was glance across the Heads toward Cheviot Beach on the Peninsula to see if the surf was smokin'. If the wind was north-easterly, she would grab her board and head for Point Lonsdale back beach.

The board she won the Australian malibu titles on – known as the Silver Shadow – was now propped up in the far corner of her Mount Martha living room. Her house was called Sea Holme; the walls were painted sky blue and sand yellow. Jan's car number plate was SURFEN. Deeply tanned and dressed in Hawaiian-style boardshorts and a luminous turquoise jacket, everything about her boldly announced that she was living her dream. I was wearing my standard inner city outfit of black and maroon, and I hadn't been for a surf for three weeks because I'd had the flu – the first of many bouts that would plague me for the next year and a half as my body absorbed the shock of the demands I was now making of it. As often happened when I was talking to committed surfers, I felt like the eternal dabbler, the dilettante, the impostor who would never divine surfing's true secrets. And then, of course, there was the writer in me who felt most at home on the edge of things, scratching at what Gerard Windsor calls 'the creative itch of alienation'.

Only two years before, I had given a paper at a literary festival about what had driven me to write *Night Surfing*. 'As an ex-surfer,' I said, 'I was writing about my passion for the ocean. But I was also writing about my sense of being an outsider in surfing culture, of knowing that I would never belong. Surfing is a skill and a way of life that I never really mastered. The bitter-sweet ache that this knowledge filled me with fuelled the writing of this novel. While I would never master the art of surfing, I realised that I could turn this sense of failure and longing into a work of art.' Freud identifies the sublimation of libidinal drives and other basic instincts through art as one of humanity's civilising 'techniques' for fending off suffering and coping with unrealised desires. Yet clearly my act of sublimation had not sufficed. That bitter-sweet ache had not been assuaged by writing *Night Surfing* and it had eventually propelled me back into the water. For all the deep satisfaction yielded by sublimation – 'an artist's joy in creating, in giving his phantasies body, or a scientist's in solving problems or discovering truths' – its intensity is mild when compared with that derived from giving full rein to the more fundamental drives. As Freud observes with palpable regret, sublimation 'does not convulse our physical being'.

On the few occasions in my late teens when I took my board out, I had so little real knowledge and understanding of the waves that learning to surf seemed impossibly difficult. Through the dim fog of my ignorance, I sensed that the only way I would improve and become more confident would be to gain practical experience in reading the ocean. Surf schools did not exist, but there was a training camp for aspiring surf lifesavers at Portsea back beach. I knew that antagonism existed between surfers and surf lifesavers and that training with the surf lifesaving club would probably only make me more of an outsider in the surfing world, but I was prepared to take the risk.

For one week, I lived in the weathered, grey clubhouse set into the side of the cliff, overlooking the water. The day began early with a two-kilometre run to the Sphinx at the eastern end of the beach and some sprints in the sand hills in the footsteps of the Olympic runner Herb Elliot who had trained in these dunes. After that, we would swim out beyond the break to a buoy and practise using the reel and line, a life-saving device that I dreaded because the line would sometimes become tangled in kelp. While I was never convinced that I could save anyone else, the physical discipline of this daily immersion along with instruction in ocean awareness – particularly how to identify a rip – and lessons in artificial respiration and first aid gave me a level of confidence I could not have gained on my own. But I knew I was there under false pretences. I did not want to be part of the club and go on patrol. What I wanted to learn were the secrets of staying alive. I also wanted somewhere to leave my board so that I would not have to lug it with me as I made my way between our beach house and the surf on foot.

Given my motives, I understood all too well why surf life-savers regarded surfers as selfish and irresponsible. The two groups began to go their separate ways after the introduction of the shorter and lighter malibu board in 1956. Surfers didn't need to store these more portable boards at clubhouses, and many of them gave up lifesaving. Historically, surf lifesaving had thrived on the Victorian-era spirit of community discipline and regimentation that continued into the postwar years. Surfing, on the other hand, was allied with the explosion of youth culture in the late 1950s and early 1960s. To surf lifesavers, surfers were hedonists bent purely on their own pleasure whose boards posed a threat to swimmers. Lifesaving, by contrast, was about community service and camaraderie, about being part of a team. Where surf lifesavers were highly regimented in their activities, surfers appeared anarchic and antisocial. Much as I could appreciate the life-savers' perspective, I was naturally drawn to surfing's more solitary individualism with its antecedents in the Romantic movement. Lifesaving's iron man ethic pitted man against nature, whereas surfing – as I saw it – was about tapping into nature's energy and rediscovering something fundamental to human existence that had been all but lost.

I could understand too why surfers regarded lifesavers as a kind of beach police. In their efforts to herd the public into the safest part of the beach, the lifesavers often placed their flags on either side of the best breaks and forbade surfers from entering this patrolled area. At Portsea, this tension took on a particular flavour that reflected the social dynamics of this end of the Peninsula. While local people helped establish the lifesaving club in 1949, most of the locals left after Portsea plumber and formation member John Wishart was taken by a shark in 1956. The city members who remained conducted recruiting drives amongst their peers from some of the top Melbourne private schools, many of whom took their holidays at Portsea, the summer playground of the city's richest families. From then on, the club was dominated by this group. In the 1960s, as surfing emerged as an expression of rebellion against the mainstream, Peninsula surfers increasingly found themselves in conflict with authority – not only with the surf lifesavers, but also with the army, which controlled all access to the beaches of Point Nepean where two of the most prized breaks on the coast were to be found.

These run-ins eventually became the stuff of local legend. One of the protagonists in this guerilla warfare was a big-limbed, cherubic-faced surfer in his early fifties called Geoff Coker who knew the coast at this end of the Peninsula better than almost anyone else. It was easy to see why younger surfers like Mark had looked up to him. He was a natural storyteller and a storehouse of local surfing lore. Much of his fishing knowledge had been passed on to him by his father, with whom Geoff had often fished. After his father died, Geoff took his old wooden boat out to the Rip, where the two had often gone together, and in heaving seas he fished for salmon and ranted to the sky, challenging the god of the waves to take him too. But if fishing had brought father and son together, surfing had been a wedge between them. Geoff's father, a returned soldier, had never been impressed with his son's long blond hair and career choice of shaping surfboards. In the postwar period, Sorrento was a conservative, RSL town; to many of its inhabitants, surfers were bad news.

No institution regarded surfers with more suspicion than the army. Point Nepean had long been a strategic location in a series of fortifications defending Port Phillip Bay and the colony of Victoria. As part of a plan to make the Heads the 'Gibraltar of the South', a fort with four eighty-pound muzzle-loading guns, a tunnel complex and barracks was built in the early 1880s. As it turned out, the only shot ever fired 'in anger' at the Heads was aimed at the German steamer *Pfalz* just after Germany and Britain went to war in August 1914. After the Second World War the fort was abandoned, but the army presence remained in the form of an officer cadet school based in the old quarantine station buildings located just inside the bay. In the absence of any real enemy, the surfers were probably the closest the officers-in-training ever got to confronting an 'infiltrating force'.

In the mid-1960s, when surfers first sought access to a surf break just inside the bay from Point Nepean which they dubbed Leprosy because of the old leper graves behind the sand dunes, the army initially allowed them to enter its territory. Geoff's brother Frank had written a formal letter to the commanding officer requesting permission to surf Leprosy, and to his amazement, permission was granted. The only condition was that the surfers stay away on days when live ammunition was being fired. Sometimes, during their excursions to Leprosy, Geoff and his friends would catch sight of awesome, hollow waves breaking at Point Nepean; but the waves were too fast for their long, unwieldy boards to handle. When shorter, seven-foot-six boards came into vogue, the surfers began venturing out to the Point, where they had the break mostly to themselves. What made the Point special (apart from the quality of the wave) was that it was the only break on either the Peninsula or the west coast that worked on a south-easterly wind.

Corsair's secret had been out for a long time now. 'It gets hugely crowded,' Geoff lamented. Because of the strong tides at the Heads, it was assumed the Point could only be surfed during the hour either side of slackwater – the lull between the tides – if one wasn't to be dragged out into Bass Strait by the ebb tide, or into the bay by the flood. 'Everyone goes there when the tide is coming in. But there's other times you can surf there when people think you can't.'

I waited for him to explain but he seemed reluctant. Even Geoff's good friends found him elusive and I was beginning to understand why. He could be forthcoming one moment, guarded the next. 'Other times?' I prodded.

'There's another slackwater when the tide is going out,' he said uneasily, as if he'd given away one of Corsair's few remaining secrets.

In the early days the other hazard at the Point was the resident twenty-foot White Pointer shark regularly spotted by the Queenscliff fishermen who regarded Geoff and his friends as mad for venturing out there. One day when the waves were a solid eight foot and backlit by the afternoon sun, the surfers saw a big, dark shape passing through a wave like a giant submarine. That was the only time they saw the shark, but it lurked in their minds like a modern-day descendant of the sea monsters marked on medieval maps.

After the prime minister Harold Holt disappeared while swimming at Cheviot Beach – one of the most treacherous ocean beaches inside the army territory – in December 1967, Geoff and his brother received a letter from the army revoking their permit. Not to be deterred, they took to walking in to the Point along the bay beaches. If they were spotted and ordered to leave, they would walk in the water, where the army officers couldn't reach them. One day they were out at a break they called Spooks, beneath the firing range, when a line of soldiers appeared on the cliff top and a sergeant with a loud hailer ordered the surfers out of the water. When they replied with the two-finger salute, the soldiers started firing into the air.

For Geoff and his mates, this guerilla warfare was just a game; they hadn't been frightened off by a Great White shark and the army wasn't going to stop them either. But if the surfers thought it a lark, the army certainly didn't. One day after surfing at the Point, Geoff and his friends returned to the beach to find their towels and belongings gone. Puzzled, they jumped into their boat and headed back to the Sorrento ramp. Just as they were easing the boat out of the water, police cars screeched to a halt with sirens blaring. The army officers had found half a Buddha stick among the towels left on the beach at Point Nepean and suspected the surfers of rendezvousing with drug-smugglers in the Rip.

Running parallel with these skirmishes was a growing mood of antagonism between surfers and surf lifesavers at Portsea over the placement of patrol flags. In the early 1970s, a stable sandbank developed in front of the clubhouse, producing exceptional waves. It was also an ideal place for swimming and was therefore patrolled. Usually, the surfers were in the water before the flags went up and resented being told to leave. When the surfers refused to move, the lifesavers would swim out and attempt to confiscate their boards. Tension had been simmering for months before it finally erupted in a brawl one hot summer's day, when the beach was thick with holidaymakers and perfect six-foot waves were peeling off the disputed sandbank. When a young surfer lost possession of his board, it was promptly seized by the lifesavers and placed inside their windbreak on the beach. A surfer built like Geronimo came out of the water fuming about the clubbies, stomped up to the windbreak and snatched the board, but not before a lifesaver grabbed the other end. A comic tug of war ensued; then Geronimo threw a punch and war began in earnest. As astounded holidaymakers looked on, surfers and clubbies came flying up from all directions, threw themselves at one another and went tumbling across the sand. By the time the police arrived, the brawl had fizzled out and the two groups had achieved a shaky truce.

Thirty years on, these confrontations were all but forgotten. The two cultures were no longer at odds and surf lifesavers were as likely to surf as anyone else.

It was a hot, glary mid-summer afternoon. I had spent the morning surfing at Jan Juc and was now back in the city at the toddler pool of the local baths where I'd taken my son for a swim. As I sat on the edge of the pool watching him wade across the pretty aqua rhomboid of water, my body was still ringing with the surf, like the pilot in Antoine de Saint-Exupéry's *Southern Mail* whose head, after he has landed, is full of the sky and the roar of the engine and whose limbs quiver from the vibrations of the plane. I only had to close my eyes for an instant to see waves rising and falling.

It had been a glorious morning's surf. Clear skies, a steady northerly and black cormorants plummeting out of the blue to disappear beneath the water before emerging seconds later with big fish flapping in their beaks. I had left Melbourne early and arrived before the worst of the crowds. Although the surf was small, the waves were glassy and kept coming at regular intervals. I could feel the hard work of earlier surfs paying off as I glided into waves that would have previously eluded me, waves that were eluding the novices nearby. It was good, for once, not to feel like a kook and to be acquiring a measure of grace. Amid the feast of waves, there was also time to sit and savour the moment, to contemplate the sky and the deeply tanned cliffs of clay and marl; to spin in lazy circles on my board and enjoy the lulls between the sets. Tiger Moths and biplanes taking sightseers on joy flights down the coast puttered back and forth overhead. For once, it was in my power to extract every ounce of sweetness the morning could yield.

Now, as I sat watching my son absorbed in the simple feat of climbing in and out of the wading pool, I found myself thinking about the inescapable tension between sea pursuits and life on land. I had been reading my son a picture book, adapted from a story by Octavio Paz, about a wave that asks a young boy at the beach to take her home. The wave floods the dark corners of the boy's house with blue and green light, and at night rocks the boy to sleep and sings sweet sea songs into the shell of his ear. But as the seasons pass, the wave feels the tug of the moon and starts to get lonely and restless, and during the long winter nights she calls up monsters from the deep. The wave is beginning to drive the boy's mother crazy and his father says the wave has to go. But they cannot catch the wave, and so the boy and his parents are forced to flee the house. During a cold snap the wave freezes, allowing the boy and his father to take her back to the sea.

This desire to bring the wild magic of the wave into one's life, and the inevitable clash between the domestic and the oceanic, are persistent themes in most sea literature. Almost all the great sea sagas, from Homer's *Iliad* onwards, are about men leaving their wives, children, lovers and the security of terra firma to fight wars, to conquer new land, to trade or to fish. Or, as in *The Odyssey*, the hero is on his way home to his wife but is constantly waylaid by sex and adventure. In Tennyson's version of Homer's epic, Ulysses no sooner gets home than he is aching to set sail once more, utterly disillusioned with the 'barren crags' of his island, his 'savage' people and his 'aged wife'. 'Come, my friends,' he says. ''Tis not too late to seek a newer world.'

The Paz story is also a kind of first love fable. The wave is feminine. She sweeps the boy off his feet, takes his hand

and together they race away across the sand. That too is typical of the seafaring genre. While women are largely absent from the archetypal sea and surf story – except as mythical figures of seduction and entrapment, or as emblems of home – the feminine principle, whether monstrous or maternal, is not. Freud believed that the oceanic feeling, as a residue of the child's 'oneness' with the mother, was 'ousted from a place in the foreground' by the role of the father as the child's protector. In the traditional sea saga, a similar displacement has occurred. The sea has become the domain of the father, even while remaining symbolically feminine. The classic rites of passage tale, where the hero goes to sea and 'becomes a name', as Tennyson's Ulysses claims, would appear to be a flight from domesticity, from all that is feminine. And yet, in truth, it is a return to the womb, as Swinburne recognises:

> I will go back to the great sweet mother,
> Mother and lover of men, the sea.
> I will go down to her, I and none other,
> Close with her, kiss her and mix her with me.

The darker side of this ecstatic union is the threat of annihilation in the belly of the all-consuming mother, a deep dread powerfully conveyed by the mesmerising, spinning vortex of the whirlpool in Edgar Allan Poe's story 'A Descent into the Maelstrom'.

Female roles in Western – as opposed to Polynesian – surfing mythology have been similar to those found in the traditional sea saga. Male surfers venture out into the waves while their girlfriends or wives, like Penelope in *The Odyssey*, remain behind. As representatives of the home and hearth, women are typically confined to the land, a tradition which surfing culture has enforced with a vengeance. 'Off went the boys into the big, blue sea,' write Gabrielle Carey and Kathy Lette in their confessional exposé of surfing subculture, *Puberty Blues*. 'Sue and I sat there on the sand . . . warming up the towel, folding his clothes into neat little piles, fetching the banana fritters and chocolate thick-shakes and watching him chuck endless re-entries.' For a girl to be accepted into a surfie gang, she had to be interested in surfing but not interested enough to surf.

On reflection, it is not surprising that the vast bulk of surfing fiction is aimed at children and adolescents, or that surfing culture has been antagonistic towards women, the archetypal symbols of domesticity. In its defiant mood of rebellion, rejection of responsibility and celebration of youth, surfing mythology celebrates the eternal adolescent in all of us: that secret part of the self that resists the civilising, domesticating process and finds atavistic solace in the sea's savage mystery. It is for this reason, perhaps, that surfing culture has a quality of arrested development which – depending on your view – can appear eternally youthful or tiresomely narcissistic.

When surfing features in mainstream novels or films, it is usually as an emblem of youthful optimism and defiance of convention. In David Malouf's novel *Fly Away Peter*, surfing is celebrated as standing for Australia's youthfulness and the New World's freedom from the past, after the bloody slaughter of the Great War sees the civilised Old World collapse into the barbarity of the trenches. 'A youth was walking – no running, on the water. Moving fast over the surface. Hanging delicately balanced there with his arms raised and his knees slightly bent as if upheld by invisible strings . . . It was new. So many things were new. Everything changed. The past would not hold and could not be held.' At the time in which Malouf's novel is set, surfing was only just taking off in Australia. But when the novel was published in 1982, its image of surfing was already nostalgic. Surfing was no longer a pristine activity free of all historical and cultural baggage. Within a few decades it had acquired its own highly exclusive mythology, which was documented with excruciating accuracy in *Puberty Blues*.

Yet when I first started surfing, it was not *Puberty Blues* I identified with, but poems like Judith Wright's 'The Surfer' and M. B. MacCallum's haunting war lyric 'Surf Time'. The surfers in these works, like the surfer in *Fly Away Peter*, were not enmeshed in the rituals or the tribal ways that had become so much a part of surfing culture and mythology: they were straight out of the Romantic tradition of the solitary figure in nature. I was drawn to this image of the lone surfer because that's how I saw myself.

From the cult film *Morning of the Earth* to recent 'big wave' thrillers like Kem Nunn's novel *The Dogs of Winter*, the dominant storyline in surfing literature, film and mythology has been the Boys' Own quest for new frontiers. What struck me now, having returned to surfing as a mature woman, was how little this narrative formula actually reflected the daily reality of most surfers' lives – and how little it reflected mine. Almost all surfers, to varying degrees, have to contend with how to combine work and family life with their surfing.

The unpredictability of the sea and the weather means that surfing can never be neatly slotted into the working week or weekend. It is also a seriously addictive passion. Initially I had assumed that surfing once a week or fortnight would be more than sufficient. Yet the more I surfed, the more I wanted; the hungrier I became. Whenever it was time to get out of the water and go home, I would keep deferring the moment with the addict's mantra, 'Just one more.' For surfers living away from the coast the balancing act was particularly delicate, and I was still grappling with how best to achieve it. While everyone set themselves personal Ithakas or Troys – mine was to surf Corsair – the more pressing, subtle and complex drama lay closer to home: the daily struggle to reconcile the domestic with the oceanic, and the tension between those two worlds.

For some surfers the problem was partially overcome by going to the surf *en famille*, but this wasn't necessarily a solution, as my partner and I discovered one muggy Sunday when we decided to give it a try. Almost as soon as we hit the Geelong freeway, our son began crying out to go home. Once at the beach, the boy wanted to follow me into the surf and I soon discovered that there was little satisfaction to be had in the water when I had to keep one eye fixed on the beach. Soon we all bundled back into the car and headed for home. My immediate reaction was disappointment, as if we had failed some crucial family test. But later I felt strangely relieved. One of the essential elements in my love of surfing was that Romantic solitariness, that sense of escape it provided from domesticity and from the responsibilities of ordinary life. Although I looked forward to the day when my son and I would go surfing together, the arrested adolescent in me was, if I was honest, quite content to go it alone, and for surfing to remain my 'other' life.

Despite these complications, surfing as a departure from domestic routine is not a major rupture; as a surfer, you *can* commune with the sublime and be home in time for tea. If we can free ourselves from the machismo of seafaring mythology, surfing allows for a new conception of adventure in which we do not need to go 'in far' in order to go 'out deep'. The beauty of surfing is that, unlike an ocean voyage, it does not require a prolonged absence. The surfer's relationship with the sea is therefore quite different from the mariner's. It is more about an endless negotiation between sea and land than the lure of the blue yonder; more about being-in-the-moment than journeying or arrival. In the end, the waves always return us to the shore, to our daily lives, and remind us that terra firma is where we belong. For all these reasons, the domestic and the oceanic can co-exist in surfing in a way that is impossible in the classic sea story; and what's more, they can enrich each other. The American writer Russell Banks compares surfing a wave to writing a short story. Stories and perfect waves, he says, 'forgive one's mercurial nature, reward one's longing for ecstasy and make of one's short memory a virtue'. As I sat watching my boy at the local baths, I knew without any doubt that my brief expeditions to the surf made me a better mother and writer. I could be content with my life in the city, with the miniature pools of the toddler enclosure and the adventure playgrounds of the local parks, because I was free to make regular forays into that larger, inexhaustible playground of the ocean.

In late February during the final sultry days of summer, we took a week's break at Sorrento. Now that the school holidays were over I hoped to surf in peace. All through January I had paid the price of surfing at the height of the holiday season – the constant hassling and mad scrabble for waves, the many bruises from collisions with other people's boards. On some days at the height of summer, the competition had been so fierce that it had been like stepping into a classroom full of whiz kids whose agility and lack of fear only emphasised my timidity and sluggishness, and whose ability to snap up the waves left me floundering around for crumbs. Far from escaping the hurly-burly of city life, I had found myself trapped in the thick of it.

Now, at around eight o'clock in the morning, I stood with my son on the clifftop, gazing out over the big blue of Portsea back beach. The forecast was for 33 degrees and it was already warm and sunny. A light off-shore wind had airbrushed away any signs of chop or agitation, varnishing the water with a high-gloss sheen. I lifted the boy above the wooden fence so that he could see the waves. Observed from such a height, waves often look deceptively small, and I remarked to a passing surfer who was heading for the stairs that there wasn't much action out there. Portsea seemed to be in an unusually lazy mood. Although waves were rolling in on two banks, there was an uncharacteristic air of calm. The surfer looked a little puzzled and then smiled forgivingly. After all, what could I be expected to know? A woman approaching forty with a toddler in tow.

As the boy and I made our way down the to beach, my attention was divided between the small black figures in the water and my son's determined efforts to descend the stairs upright 'like a big boy', rather than backwards on his belly. Our progress was inevitably slow. When we reached the beach no one was about, but parallel to the sea the freshly washed sand was already imprinted with a broken ribbon of human and dog prints, which was intersected by the slantwise tracks of surfers heading for the water. Suddenly agitated by the whoosh and surge of the sea, my son cried out, 'No, Mama, no,' and turning on his heel, yanked me back towards the stairs. I glanced over my shoulder to see a surfer sliding into a perfect left-hander – a wave breaking from left to right – then gleefully working his way across the translucent surface that kept hollowing beneath his feet as if responding to his command. Just before the blue wall dissolved into foam, the surfer flicked his board skyward. As he slipped smoothly over the back of the wave, I could almost hear him sighing with satisfaction.

It was after ten o'clock by the time I left my son with his father and returned to Portsea with my board. The surf had picked up, but the water had lost its pristine, early morning sheen and there were now at least ten surfers vying for the waves. For once, it was ridiculously easy to paddle out. Arriving at the line-up always made me feel self-conscious, as if I was stepping into a room full of strangers. I had planned to hang back and study the waves for a while, but a set was approaching and even as the other surfers let the first wave go, I sensed that with a few extra strokes it could be mine. To my surprise, I was right. I could almost hear a 'click' as everything slipped into place. This was what Jack had meant when he talked about the importance of being decisive, of not hanging back; it gave you a psychological edge, not so much over the other surfers as over the insecure, doubting side of yourself. Everything felt strangely effortless as the wave picked me up and I rose to my feet. From then on, it was if a spell had been cast over the water, the waves unspooling like liquid celluloid as I floated across their flickering walls, grinning with disbelief. I'd never experienced anything like this before: waves that kept peeling and then reforming and hollowing out as if they might never end.

Emboldened, I decided to try manoeuvring the board, cutting back into the foaming lip to prolong the ride, marvelling at the way the wave itself seemed to guide me in these basic steps, like a parent taking a child's hand. How simple and clear it all suddenly seemed. *This* was how it was supposed to be. *This* was what it was all about. While I'd had occasional moments of revelation akin to this when surfing many years ago, they had always seemed like flukes, like one-offs that I couldn't hope to repeat. But this was different. The usual feeling of precariousness, the feeling that I was hanging in there by the skin of my teeth was replaced by a much more fluid sense of concord; a sense that I was acting *with* the wave rather than being acted *upon*. I knew I had to hold on to this sensation of discovery, this joy of learning how to walk again. When I paddled back out to the line-up, all the other surfers seemed to be smiling at me – perhaps because I was now smiling at them.

Towards the Heads, the pillar of the Point Lonsdale light-house and the tiny, far-off houses along the west coast glowed in the sunlight like whitewashed cubes on a Greek island. I got talking to a seasoned, square-jawed surfer sitting on a malibu. David had recently returned to the Peninsula after ten years in the United States. I asked him whether he had been struck by the changes that had taken place during his absence. You only had to take a glance at the Portsea cliff line: the land behind the narrow strip of national park had been opened up for development not long ago, putting an end to the fragile illusion of wilderness that this coastline had once afforded. From where we sat in the water you could now see the top section of a house – a big, glass-fronted thing like the flagship of an invading fleet – poking up from the other side of the dunes. In the past ten years this end of the Peninsula had gone from being a quiet, modestly pretty seaside town which briefly flared into life each summer to a gentrified, self-consciously charming, all-year-round holiday resort. Every scrap of available land seemed to have been subdivided for further development, with more and more chunky, grandiose houses looming above the treeline. The hourly and sometimes half-hourly car ferry from Queenscliff ensured that boatloads of day-trippers poured into the township at regular intervals. And every summer, the crowds and traffic jams grew worse. I had begun to wonder if the subdivisions and new apartments would continue to multiply until the human density on this fragile tip of land became as high as the inner city suburb in which I lived. Only the very wealthy few with their large beachfront estates could escape the crush.

David agreed that a lot had changed. The way he said it suggested that he was talking as much about his own life as about the changes around us. It was evident that he commanded the respect of the other surfers, not because he hassled vigorously or attempted to dominate the waves but because he refused to be swept up in the competitive scrabbling that is endemic to most line-ups. He happily let others take waves that could easily have been his. When I agonised over my stance and earnestly quizzed him about it, he was reluctant to comment. Everyone had their own style, he said when pressed. The important thing was to enjoy being in the water and to take each wave as it came. It was deceptively simple advice, the wisdom of which I was slow to absorb.

The anticipation, the shared affinity with the sea, the temporary sense of being cut loose from ordinary life could create a confessional mood in the surf. One sunny day at Jan Juc a surfer told me about his daughter's struggle with muscular dystrophy and of her death at the age of twelve. More often than not, though, conversations out the back were cryptic and fragmented, disrupted by the unpredictable behaviour of the swell. I never found out what had brought David back to the Peninsula. The waves rolled in and the mood was broken.

Hanging in the kitchen at Sorrento was a photograph, taken in the 1920s, of the surf at the back beach. I could tell from the clean lines of swell, the way the waves were peeling rather than crumbling and the lack of white water and chop that the wind on that day had been off-shore, probably a north-easterly. It was such a basic deduction for a surfer that it was easy to forget that it was not general knowledge. I was slowly developing a connoisseur's eye for waves. But there was still much that I was blind to in the surf and much that I would probably never see; my education in learning to read the ocean, which formally began when I trained for my surf lifesaving bronze, would be an apprenticeship without end.

The art of understanding the waves at Portsea (and all beach breaks) lay mostly in learning to fathom the shape and nature of the sand bank below, the hidden template upon which the contours of each wave were built. While knowledge of this kind helped surfers understand what to expect from the waves they were riding, it was even more vital to surf life-savers: it could mean the difference between life and death for swimmers under their guard. One summer's day at Portsea in the late 1950s, when the surf was very heavy and the beach crowded, a surf lifesaver called Malcolm Hall looked out over the water and sensed that the sandbar over which everyone was swimming was about to collapse. He knew that if this happened, a strong rip would start to run and hundreds of swimmers would be swept out to sea. Most of the club members were at a carnival on the west coast and there were only six lifesavers patrolling the beach. Realising they weren't enough to cope with a mass rescue, Hall organised two reels to be unwound and their lines towed out beyond the swimmers. The belts were then fixed together, forming a giant lasso. When the sandbar gave way mid-afternoon, as he had feared it would, sweeping swimmers off their feet and dragging many of them out of their depth, Hall ordered the lines to be reeled in, as if rounding up a runaway herd of cattle. Every swimmer was hauled in safely thanks to his feeling for the sea floor.

That week, I had no idea what was happening to the sand-bar below me, except that it had produced the most wonderful waves I had ever had the good fortune to ride. On the third day, when it was time to get home to my son, I caught a wave just as it was peaking. Like a gracious host seeing me to the door after a three-day feast, it delivered me all the way to the beach. I waded from the water, flicked the leg rope around the tail, tucked the board under my arm and headed for the stairs. I'd just had the surf of my life and things could only get better. At this rate, I would be surfing at Point Nepean before the end of the year.

CHAPTER 3

Skimming the Abyss

AUTUMN

Exultation is the going
Of an inland soul to sea,
Past the houses – past the headlands –
Into deep Eternity

Emily Dickinson, 'Exultation is the going'

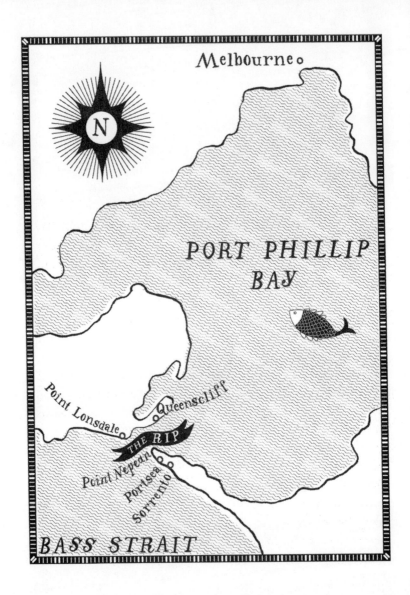

Melbourne○

N

PORT PHILLIP
BAY

Point Lonsdale

Queenscliff

THE RIP

Point Nepean

Portsea

Sorrento

BASS STRAIT

A MOOD OF autumnal dreaminess hung over Port Phillip Bay like a watercolour wash as we walked down the concrete pier toward the silvery, skeletal metropolis of the Brighton marina. Beyond the horizon lay the full sweep of the two peninsulas that form the bay, and between them, our destination: the Rip. I could almost feel that narrow body of water drawing me toward it like a magnetic pole. For most sailors, the Rip was a gap, an opening, an entrance to be negotiated and passed through, not a destination. But in my mind, it was a place in itself; ever-mysterious, ever-changing. One of those enigmatic zones, like the Bermuda Triangle, that can seem a gateway to another world.

John Bryson worked on disengaging the boat – a 33-foot motor catamaran called *Huia* after his great-grandmother – from its moorings, setting the instruments and checking on the broken pump in the toilet. When we started motoring slowly away from the pier, our illuminated path began to etch itself across the chart of the bay on the small screen of the satellite plotter in the cabin. The smell of the motor fuel mingled with the acrid, briny whiff of the water as the city disappeared into a smoggy haze.

When I first met John at the end of 1994, I associated him with the desert, not the sea. He was famous for his extraordinary book, *Evil Angels*, about the disappearance of the baby Azaria Chamberlain at Uluru and Lindy Chamberlain's conviction for the murder of her daughter. We were doing a reading together at a small bar in the city. John was dressed in a cream linen suit that made him look like a character out of a Somerset Maugham story, an impression reinforced by his deep, measured voice and gentlemanly manner. After the reading, I told him that I had recently been out at night on a pilot boat through the Heads, doing research for my novel *Night Surfing*. He said that if I ever wanted to go out on the bay, I should let him know.

Ever since taking up surfing as a teenager, I had regarded the bay with something approaching disdain. It was merely a means to an end, a big pond, a watery limbo between me and the real sea – Bass Strait. Although plenty of Melbourne surfers learned to surf in the bay, especially around Brighton when a howling south-westerly whipped up the water to produce something resembling a wave, I could not summon much interest in this ersatz surf. Intrinsic to the thrill of surfing had always been the act of fleeing the city, of stepping over the horizon and into another world.

This trip across the bay with John was an act of reconnaissance, of familiarisation; a glimpse into the future, to appraise my chances of surfing at Point Nepean, and a journey into the past, into the layers of myth that made the Rip much more than the mouth of the bay. Describing his voyage around the tip of the Californian peninsula into the Gulf of California, John Steinbeck wrote of the atavistic, 'Scylla-Charybdis fear' that is connected with such 'half-mythical' places; a fear that 'made our ancestors people such place with monsters and enter them only after prayer and propitiation'. It was my hope that by confronting my fear of the Rip, I might dispel it.

A light north-easterly wind ruffled the smoky-blue sheet of the bay and edged the clouds away to the south. All autumn it had been like this – clear, amber days with gentle, off-shore breezes. In thirty-eight years of living in Melbourne, I had skirted the bay by car, swum on its fringes and paid scant attention to its hidden interior. Now it was as though John and I had stepped through a looking glass and were gazing back on the city from the other side. Far from being a 'big pond', the bay seemed to have no end. Lost in a haze, the shrunken, distant skyscrapers belonged to another epoch, another life. It was suddenly easy to imagine a time when the bay was a grassy plain, through which the ancestral Yarra River wended its way towards Bass Strait during the last ice age, seventy-five thousand years ago.

That fertile basin, where fish now swam, had once been the hunting ground of the tribes of the Kulin nation. The last inundation of the area, which took place ten thousand years ago, is recorded in their myths. One myth tells of two little boys hurling toy spears at each other as they imitate their fathers. A spear goes awry and upsets a magical wooden trough which contains a tremendous amount of water. The water gushes over the land and threatens to drown all the people. However, Bunjil, the Creator, takes pity on them. He controls the path of the water by putting a rock where Mornington now lies, and two more at the Heads, and then directing the water to flow between them to meet the ocean. In another myth, the water of the Yarra is locked in the mountains in a gigantic lake called Moorool, or 'great water', which has consumed the hunting grounds of the Woiwurong tribe. The headman, Bar-wool, and one of his tribesmen cut channels through the valley with their stone axes, making their way slowly toward the coast. Eventually the freed waters of Moorool rush out, releasing the country of the Woiwurong but flooding the plains of Port Phillip, the hunting ground of the Bunurongs.

In these myths, the inundation is sudden rather than gradual, the water bursting across the landscape like waters breaking from a womb. As well as recording, in compressed, poetic form, the geological history of the area, these stories also capture the fury of the twice-daily passage of the tides through the narrow gateway of the Heads: the release of dammed-up water at ebb tide, the ocean forcing its way back into the bay with the flood.

*

On the console behind the wheel, the compass bobbed in its glass dome. The red bluffs of Indented Head should be visible by now, John said. If we held to 210°, they would soon come up.

'Come up?' I smiled at the idea of it. He made it sound as if our approach was conjuring up the cliffs out of the haze.

'Well, if you think about it, sea navigation works a lot like an Aboriginal song-cycle. If you sing the song correctly, it creates the topography as you travel in a certain direction over a certain distance. You sing up a mountain, or you sing up a waterhole. What's interesting about the process is that it takes the traveller's point of view. It doesn't say, "Do this and you will come to a waterhole." It says, "Do this and the waterhole will come to you." When you look at the official sailing tomes which tell navigators what to expect – reefs, beaches, islands – the same orientation applies. If you stay at a compass bearing of such and such and a speed of such and such, your course will bring up on your port bow the island of . . . '

'Atlantis?'

He smiled. 'The island of Atlantis. But we're talking real landmarks here. It's the same in the song-cycles. You're not looking at the landscape dispassionately. It's as if you're creating the landscape by doing certain things well.'

Aboriginal song-cycles map the ocean as well, through secular and sacred 'seamarks'. The seamarks of the saltwater people of the Australian tropics, for instance, include islands, reefs, dugong areas, sandbars, deep-water areas, rocks where pelicans sleep, and tidal currents which they call 'roads in the sea'. Like the Polynesian navigators of old, the saltwater people of the tropics knew how to read the stars, the movements of sea birds, and the degree of phosphorescence in the water (which could indicate depth) in order to find their way around.

Polynesian navigators also learned to read the ocean from the way the vibrations of the swell registered in their bodies. On their stick charts made of pandanus reed, with shells marking the location of atolls and islands, lines and curves represent swells from different directions and how they are refracted by the islands. These wave patterns charted the way the water looked to a navigator standing in the bow of a canoe and also functioned as a navigation 'notebook'. Each chart reflected the perspective and knowledge of a particular navigator, and would inevitably differ from another man's chart of the same area.

I had no nautical skills whatsoever. Yet, in my own way, I, too, was creating a private sea chart. Through this expedition with John, and through encounters with those who knew the bay intimately – pilot boat captains, surfers, divers, marine biologists and fishermen – I hoped to navigate the tangle of forbidding yet seductive stories that clung to the Rip like a forest of kelp. Whereas ancient mariners entered strange waters armed with their faith, I was trying to arm myself with knowledge. Not that I expected to know the Rip well. Just well enough to reach some understanding of what I was up against. Just well enough to begin to imagine my way into the waves that came surging through the Heads bringing news of a storm in distant latitudes before they met their fate on the sandbar at Point Nepean.

I had been here before in my imagination when writing *Night Surfing*. But back then I'd had the power of Bunjil; I was a god commanding the tides to change and unleashing a south-westerly gale as my young protagonist, Jake, attempted to surf at the Point. To shift from the perspective of an omnipotent author of fiction to that of an Aboriginal or Polynesian navigator standing in the bow of his craft was to be forcefully reminded of the abyss between words and actions, between dreaming and doing.

John's mother was part-Maori — as a young boy, John had visited his Maori aunts in Sydney — and he suspected that his father had Maori blood too. When John was about ten years old, he announced to their housekeeper that his family were Maori. The housekeeper was not impressed and neither was John's father, who thrashed him with a skipping rope to make sure that he did not speak of his Maori heritage again. At the time, his father was struggling to establish himself in the business community and was fearful of the stigma attached to a non-white background.

A speed boat flew like a silver arrow across the water towards a gaggle of others like it in the distance.

'There might be a race on today,' John mused. The prospect brought with it a raft of memories. His father used to race speed boats in Sydney and his younger brother, Hugh, who loved speed of all kinds, had been a keen competitor on the bay. John himself had flirted with car racing in the late 1950s during his final years at university studying law. He stripped out the Jaguar sports XK 140 that his father had bought him, turned it into a racing car and took it to the race circuit on Phillip Island. One day he was hurtling around the track when he came to a stretch with a magnificent view over Bass Strait. It was a beautiful day and an ocean yacht race was taking place. The spinnakers were up and the sight made him wonder what he was doing inside this open bullet, exhausted from being up all night fixing the engine, his face covered in grit, while out there on the water people were racing and having fun. When he got home that night, he told his father that he was going back to sailing.

Hugh's appetite for speed was much greater. At twenty-one, he was killed while on his way to a race in Surfers Paradise. For John, Hugh would forever be a 'flash sort of kid', who loved nothing better than to be in a large fast boat full of good-looking women.

Clumsily I asked, 'Were you very close to your brother?'

His reply was a pained grunt. 'Yes.'

There were no clear rules for this kind of navigation, this delicate business of sounding out the submerged landscape of someone else's past.

We were now off Queenscliff, motoring steadily towards the Heads. I had met a fisherman in Queenscliff who knew the topography of the Rip as well as he knew the surrounding countryside. At seventy-six, Lewis Ferrier still lived in the small fisherman's cottage where he had grown up. In his head was a map of this submerged landscape as it had been before the great deluge, when birds flew where fish now swam and the people of the Kulin nation camped and hunted there. The circumstances of Lewis's birth were so auspicious they might have been conceived by Gabriel García Márquez. He was born on the front beach next to the main pier in December 1924, his entrance hastened by the exertions of his mother, who had joined a crowd of locals helping the fishermen haul in a record catch of salmon. When her husband caught sight of her pulling on the ropes, he urged her to go home. Frances Ferrier was still making her way up the beach when her waters broke and she went into labour. By the time the local midwife arrived, Lewis's sandy head was resting on his mother's knee.

John pointed out Shark Alley, also known as the Swashaway, which runs between Point Lonsdale and the semi-exposed Lonsdale Reef. Jack Finlay had told me of the limestone caves on the ocean side of the Point Lonsdale lighthouse which reminded him of the 'caverns measureless to man' in Coleridge's 'Kubla Khan'. And of the school of Australian salmon which once swam around him there like a silver carousel, a spinning wall so high and thick that he couldn't see through it. Jack's hoard of diving memories were like glittering fragments of poetry or snatches of dreams that he had brought back from the depths along with the old doorknobs, bits of glass decanters and other sea-worn objects he had plucked from the wrecks of sailing ships before fossicking was made illegal.

Beneath us now was what was known as the Lonsdale Wall, a rocky platform which flanked the western side of the gorge created by the ancestral Yarra. Hidden from our sight was a series of terraced escarpments covered with kelp and an assortment of remarkable organisms – brightly coloured sponges, huge bryozoans or sea-lace and brain-like sea squirts – which filtered the 'fast food' carried by the rapid currents travelling in and out of the Rip.

An orange and black pilot boat chugged purposefully past, heading for the Queenscliff marina. As I watched, I thought of Captain Mike Carolin, the sea pilots' unofficial historian. The day I met him at their head office in North Melbourne, he spread out a shipping map of the Heads on the table in front of us and spoke solemnly of the enormous pressure created there by the tides: either the whole of Bass Strait is trying to pour in through the narrow entrance at the Heads or the one thousand nine hundred and fifty square kilometres of water in the Bay is trying to force its way out. Every six hours the incoming or outgoing tides squeeze through the Heads at up to eight knots, but it takes three hours before the water in the bay and in the strait level out. For instance, during the first three hours of a *flood* tide, the water is actually travelling *out* of the bay.

Whenever the wind and the tide were travelling in opposite directions, the Rip became a battleground of contending forces, said Mike. With every ebb tide, water flowing out of the bay collided with the powerful Southern Ocean swell that had been rolling unimpeded for thousands of kilometres. The impact could create peaks of up to five metres. The sudden changes in depth of the sea floor here, together with the force of the tides, created swirling currents and whirlpools that could spin a small craft around – if it hadn't already been swamped by the surf.

'When Harold Holt got lost only about a mile from the Heads he was swimming in a rock basin full of kelp and currents and swirling surf. Afterwards, people said, "You'd have to be mad to go swimming there." But they go out at Point Nepean, where conditions are the same.'

Mike spoke with the controlled exasperation of someone who had seen too many damn fools on the water. Along with his neatly clipped beard, it was this quiet, steely authority that marked him out as a sea captain. What he said next made me glad I hadn't told him that I hoped to surf Corsair.

'It might be all right for very experienced surfers, but you get these kids who have been surfing for a couple of years and think they have enough experience to handle it. How there haven't been more deaths . . . ' He didn't need to finish the sentence.

Most of the deaths at the Heads in the last fifty years had been caused by yachting and small boat accidents. Now there were jet-skiers everywhere, a 'recipe for disaster' according to Mike. One day he was bringing a tanker in through the Heads when three jet-skis came out of nowhere and hugged the sides of the ship so closely that they couldn't be seen from the bridge. They were hovering around the bow to watch the propeller.

'If they fell off,' Mike sighed, 'they'd go straight through it like meat in a mincer.'

It would take just one death in the Rip to make a front page story. Yet when two hundred and twenty boat people had recently disappeared in the waters between Australia and Indonesia during a monsoonal storm, the response in Australia was muted, almost indifferent. There were no graphic television images of the disaster; for most of us, those deaths might never have happened.

John quietly announced that we were now in the Rip. I peered disbelievingly over the edge of the boat. The Rip is an S-shaped gorge carved by the ancestral Yarra river. The edge of the Nepean Bank, on the Point Nepean side, plunges from eleven metres to fifty metres. Within the gorge itself there is a sudden drop from about fifty metres to ninety-four, suggesting that this section of the river, which is called the Abyss, was once a waterfall. As an abyss, it is a very modest one when compared with the great submarine canyons found beyond the edges of continental shelves, or the five-mile-deep chasm into which the intrepid Elstead descends in his huge ball of steel in H. G. Wells's science fiction story 'In the Abyss'. Even so, ninety-four metres is a long way down. All I could see was dark blue water, the surface lightly cross-hatched with currents and gently grazed by the wind. The water was so calm – only the slightest sign of the flood tide disturbing the surface and the occasional faint surge of swell – that all the stories about the treachery of the Rip seemed exaggerated or fanciful. I spotted a few small whirlpools, circles of deceptive calm, but there was little evidence of swirling currents. My image of the Abyss was based on a hydrographic model of the Rip at the Queenscliff Maritime Museum, and as I stared down at the opaque water, I could not bring the toy-sized model in my head to life. What lay below remained steadfastly unfathomable.

The boat slipped along with disconcerting ease and suddenly we were in Bass Strait. I had been expecting something more momentous, a sense of arrival, of having made a *passage*. In a way, it was like meeting a notoriously violent person whose handshake turns out to be limp and manner impassive; only the occasional, flickering expression betrays the mood swings and explosions of fury for which he is known.

John spun the wheel. We headed back towards Point Nepean, which is regarded as the more dangerous side of the Rip because the tides and currents are much stronger there. The water travels in an anti-clockwise direction within the bay and, after passing through the submarine gorge known as Entrance Deep, diverts to the south-east as it flows out through the Heads. It has been said that the strong tides thus produced provide a perfect means for disposing of unwanted bodies. In the late 1970s a man who was later to become an infamous inmate of Pentridge prison wrapped the body of one of his victims in chains and chickenwire, took it out in a boat and dumped it overboard near the Heads. Afterwards, he boasted about this foolproof method of disposal, unaware that he had misjudged the tides. The body was found washed ashore at Point Lonsdale two weeks later. If he had dumped it closer to Point Nepean, it might have been a different story.

Of the eighty-five ships that have been wrecked around the

Heads, most met their fate on the Nepean side, especially around the submerged rock pinnacle of Corsair. It is a doubly fitting name: the rock was first charted by the pilot cutter *Corsair*, and lies in waiting, like a corsair or pirate, ready to snare the unsuspecting. The area is so treacherous that the sea pilots have their own channel on the Point Lonsdale side. While large ships are advised to keep clear, fishermen and small craft can pass through the shallow channel between Corsair Rock and the Nepean Reef.

For all the sea pilot's knowledge of the topography of the Rip, his task is largely a linear one – to keep to the channel lines designated for large tankers. High on the bridge of the ship, eight or ten storeys up, he is far removed from the turbulence of the water surface and the submarine world beneath it. Down among the spume and the spray, the fisherman's perspective on the Rip is inevitably more intimate and three dimensional. In order to find the fish, he must be able to envisage the sea floor, its escarpments and pinnacles, sandbanks and reefs.

Long before depth sounders were invented, fishermen charted the sea floor with the aid of a weighted pyramid of lead suspended on two hundred feet of fine line. The lead would be smothered in dripping and dropped to the bottom to measure the depth of the water. When the lead was hauled up, the fishermen could tell from the indentations and debris on the dripping what kind of ground lay below. The lead became an extension of the fisherman's fingertips: it was his way of 'feeling' the bottom. He was usually searching for reef with kelp and other vegetation for crayfish or sharks to feed on. A sandy bottom was like a submarine desert: there was little chance of finding fish there. Today, a fisherman has only to flick the switch of the depth sounder and an image of the sea floor appears before his eyes.

John was careful to stay clear of Corsair Rock as we looped back into the bay and finally approached Point Nepean from the north. It was a strange sight – the south-easterly swell gently rolling in through the Heads then pivoting at 90° before surging towards the Point. With the wind cross-shore, I did not expect to see anyone out in the water. Looking across the narrow tip of the Peninsula, I could see clean waves breaking on the Bass Strait beaches; on a day like this, with a light north-easterly wind, most surfers would head straight to the beaches between Gunnamatta and Portsea. Suddenly I noticed the silver glint of a tin runabout whisking out over the hump of a wave and two small black figures nearby. From our position behind the waves, we could see the head of one of the surfers about to make the drop. Then he disappeared behind the surging bank of water. The small craft was towing the surfers into the waves so that they didn't have to fight the flood tide to get back to the line-up.

If the wind had been blowing from the south-east, there would have been a lot more surfers out; in those conditions, there could be fifty or more surfers competing for the waves. It was the only surf break that surfers from both the Mornington and Bellarine peninsulas could lay claim to.

United and yet divided by the Rip, it was here that the rivalry between the east and west coasts was most keenly felt. In the recollections of staunch Mornington Peninsula loyalist Geoff Coker, east coast surfers had 'this pristine wave' to themselves until one day in the early 1970s when a boat arrived from the west and the occupants 'weren't friendly'. Thirty years on, Geoff's vehemence remained undiminished. He still spoke of that boat as of a foreign invasion.

'All of a sudden, it was competition time. It started to get a bit ugly in the water because the west coast is an incredibly aggressive coast. I wouldn't surf there if it was the last place on earth. I'd rather give up surfing. It's too cut-throat, dog-eat-dog – both the surfing industry there and the surfers. Still to this day, the west coast blokes come over, jump in at Quarantine and all of a sudden there's tension in the air.'

Point Lonsdale surfer Barry Orvis laughed about this rivalry. 'They always claimed that it was their break because it was on their coast. We always claimed that it was ours because we could see it from home. We'd walk up to Rip View and you could see the swell and the waves and off you'd go. It was only three kilometres away, much closer to us than to anyone on the Peninsula. Their argument was probably better, but we didn't ever let them know that.'

There was one thing that Geoff Coker and Barry Orvis agreed on. Echoing Captain Mike Carolin, they both found it amazing that no surfers had come to grief at Corsair.

*

As we skirted the coast, heading for Sorrento, I found myself playing the tour guide, pointing out landmarks of historical interest, conscious that this was not John's side of the bay. We spied the fortifications at Point Nepean, a reminder of Australia's longstanding and largely unfounded fear of invasion, which began with the Crimean War in the 1850s. The most recent echo of this fear could be heard in the dire predictions about Australia being overrun by boat people, as if they were an enemy force. As ABC journalist Peter Mares observes in *Borderlines*, 'We are warned that we are in danger of being "swamped" by "a flood tide" of "illegal immigrants" (or simply "illegals"). They threaten to "inundate us" in "waves", and even in "tsunamis".' What these metaphors captured, apart from our fear of invasion, was an uneasiness about the way our coastline exposed us to the uncontrollable power of the sea.

Further on, John and I passed the former quarantine station – an early detention centre for the sick. Once we reached Portsea, the landmarks were of a very different kind: mostly the shimmering, grand holiday homes of the rich, including George Coppin's limestone house on the hill overlooking the Sorrento jetty.

John said, 'I gather you'd like to live here one day.'

The waterfront mansions of Melbourne's wealthiest families glided by like confections from the world of Gatsby. I watched them, mesmerised.

'I don't think I could,' I finally confessed. 'It wouldn't be the same if I lived here all the time. I'd probably end up hating it – and then I'd have nowhere I could escape to.'

We motored parallel with the Sorrento front beach – the beach of my childhood – and a sudden rush of possessiveness swept over me as the Peninsula curved before us like a giant cradle. Many of my happiest and most intense memories were contained within this hummocky arc of land. In 'South of My Days', Judith Wright describes her 'blood's country', the tablelands of New England where she grew up: 'the high lean country / full of old stories that still go walking in my sleep.' One of these stories is about Old Dan, the drover: 'Seventy years of stories he clutches round his bones. / Seventy summers are hived in him like old honey.' *Hived in him like old honey*. It was a line that rang in my head whenever I savoured the memories Sorrento had given me. They were hived in me like old honey – an inexhaustible store of sweetness I could draw on whenever I had the need.

Yet they were the memories of a child on her summer holidays who gives no thought to the complex layers of human history that are embedded in the landscape she loves. Only since I had started to contemplate the geological history of this area and its history prior to European settlement had I begun to think of the fate of the first inhabitants of this area, the Bunurong clan of the Kulin people. And even now my impulse was to veer away from it, to say that it was not part of *my* story. What did it have to do with me that fifty years after Sorrento was first settled in 1803, the Bunurong tribe was wiped out? In 'Nigger's Leap, New England', a poem about the Aboriginal men, women and children who were driven over a cliff into the sea in a revenge killing in New England, Judith Wright warns against the impulse to dissociate ourselves from these events: the past is a wave with the potential to wreck us if we ignore it.

> Night buoys no warning
> over the rocks that wait our keels; no bells
> sound for her mariners . . .
> Night floods us suddenly as history
> that has sunk many islands in its good time.

Whether I liked it or not, my summer migrations to the coast contained a ghostly echo of the Bunurong people's migrations down the Peninsula each summer to camp at Sorrento. They collected shellfish from the rock platforms around Point Nepean, which they called *Boonatallung* – 'the stretched skin of the kangaroo' – before making their way up the country along the Bass Strait coast. The canoes they used for fishing in rivers and possibly around the shores of the bay were made from a single sheet of bark stripped from a tree with a stone hatchet and shaped over a fire. While these canoes were stable enough for a man to stand in and spear a fish, it is thought unlikely that they were used in the open waters of the bay or in Bass Strait. There is no evidence that the Kulin people discovered the pleasures of surfing as the Polynesians did when out fishing in their much sturdier, ocean-going craft.

It was only now, as I disembarked at the sailing club jetty at Sorrento, that I had that sense of having made a *passage*. The great 'empty' space of the bay was no longer empty for me, nor was it simply a world unto itself: the bay brought the Rip and its history to my urban doorstep. The same water that broke in waves upon the ocean beaches and surged through the Heads lapped the shores of the bayside beaches and meandered up the Yarra. It was one thing to know this intellectually but another to have experienced the connections for myself. I thanked John for making this series of small revelations possible and waved goodbye from the jetty as he began motoring back towards the distant outline of the city. We had been gone only four hours, yet out on the bay, time had stretched beyond measure.

Just before dusk that evening, my son and I went to Portsea back beach for a walk. About five surfers were having a feast on some solid, cleanly breaking waves further up the beach. In my surf-starved state I couldn't keep my eyes off them. Up behind London Bridge, the sky looked like something Turner might have painted – the low cloud a swirling mass of incandescent red and orange.

One of the reasons for my state of starvation was that I had been sick. A bout of the flu had kept me out of the water in early autumn, and from then on, every time I surfed I came down with a cold. This had been going on for months, leaving me constantly tired. One day, in the local supermarket, I ran into a friend who extravagantly announced, 'Whenever I think of you, I see you on a wave with your hair blowing back behind you, totally free.' Her image of me was so far removed from the reality of my life over recent months that I could only laugh. I hadn't been for a surf for weeks – just the thought of it made me feel exhausted – and if I was honest, I had to admit that things had started to go awry even before I came down with the flu.

Over the summer, in a haphazard, almost imperceptible way, an irrational kind of deadline fever had taken hold of me. Having made up my mind that I was going to surf at least once a week, I had inadvertently created a routine that I felt bound to stick by, goaded by the fear that I wasn't 'serious' if I did not. Convinced that the only way to avoid the crowds in the water was to surf as early as possible, I was constantly racing the clock, charging down the Geelong freeway as if I was running late for work. I had become obsessed with improvement. If I wanted to surf Corsair, I told myself, I had to make progress at a steady rate. But, of course, it didn't happen like that. Too much was out of my control – the weather, the waves, the distance to the surf. Early on, in one of my more beatific moments, I had scribbled in my notebook that *surfing teaches you how to find pleasure in endless flux and how to live with what you can't control*. If surfing had taught me this, it was a lesson that I had swiftly forgotten and was clearly going to have to relearn over and over again.

This is not to deny the magical, unforgettable days; the days when everything came together, when I was content with my ability such as it was. But more recently, the experience had fallen miserably short because I was expecting too much. After the high-water mark of those three glorious days at Portsea at the end of February when I felt that I had finally joined the ranks of the 'real' surfer, I seemed to be going backwards. Instead of feeling refreshed after a session, all I could think about were the waves I had missed or had fallen off or had failed to make the most of. Or, occasionally, the surfers who had hassled me if I got in their way. The low point came one sunny morning at Point Impossible on the west coast, where the locals gave no quarter and an old bloke on a malibu snarled at me for 'dropping in' (taking off on a wave that was technically his). He then proceeded to hog every wave while relishing my failure to get a decent ride. I drove back along the freeway with teeth clenched and fingers rigid on the wheel. By the time I got home I was a storm cloud about to break.

It was crazy that it had come to this. I might as well have been surfing in a wave-making machine, so narrow had my focus become, so little was I enjoying the total experience – the many pleasures of *being in the water*, the intense arousal of all the senses, the sheer adventure of it all. Somehow I had turned every surf into a training session for a self-imposed examination that I dared not fail. And it wasn't only my surfing that was suffering. For a time, writing too lost its magic. Nothing flowed. I would sit at my desk for hours without a break, squeezing out words and erasing them before heading home as grim-faced as when I returned from a surf. Each day foolishly digging myself a little bit deeper into my own little abyss.

What's the rush? I said aloud to myself as my son and

I walked slowly along the sand, which was littered with long black and white seabird feathers so big you could have used them as a quill. Since becoming a mother I'd just begun – for the first time in my life – to learn the meaning of patience and the joys of idling; the consolations of cyclical time; the eternal return of biological and natural rhythms; the acceptance of a slower pace. But already I had slipped back into my old hasty, impatient habits. Always wanting to make 'progress', wanting to be moving on. 'The time of departure, of transport and arrival,' says Julia Kristeva, 'is what psychoanalysts would call "obsessional time".' How quickly I had lost sight of surfing's most supreme pleasures – the immersion in the here and now, and, simultaneously, in what Kristeva calls 'monumental time', which is 'all-embracing and infinite'. If the eroding shoreline is regarded as a barometer of constant flux, the vast blue of the open ocean is an image of its opposite: eternity staring us in the face. And where sea and land collide, the ocean as an image of eternity takes on a mortal, human dimension. Time cannot be held, but when the energy silently coursing through deep water finally explodes upon the shore in a burst of white noise, the eternal becomes the now. Every wave is a perfect expression of the present tense: it can't be grasped or prolonged, only ridden.

My son had started collecting the feathers, and together we placed them on the top of little castles in the sand while I kept one eye on the action in the water. I was glad to find that I could enjoy watching the surfers swoop and glide across the burnished surface of the waves and not feel agitated that I was unable to join them. A small sign, perhaps, that I was starting to get things in perspective again. I turned back to my son, knowing that I could not afford to take my eyes off him for too long with the shorebreak surging high up the beach with the incoming tide. As if to illustrate my fears, a rogue wave swirled out of nowhere and wrapped itself around the ankles of a toddler and a young girl playing ball with their parents on the sand nearby. The children tottered in their sodden trousers, squealing with horrified delight. Luckily their parents were close enough to seize them before the wave could whip them into the sea. Within seconds, nothing remained of the wave's explosive and potentially lethal energy but a kind of photo-graphic negative – a dissolving, filigreed outline of scalloped foam on the sand.

As the boy and I made our way back to the carpark, two young surfers decided to go out. There were no decent waves breaking on the usual bank to the left of the clubhouse. Yet something had lured them in, something had inspired them to take their chances before darkness fell. The air had turned to chiffon with the dusk. Before leaving, I stood at the cliff top with my son squirming in my arms and watched the surfers struggling in the shorebreak as the sun disappeared behind London Bridge. In the hazy light, the puce-colored ocean looked vaster than ever and as strange and uninhabitable as a distant planet. Rising and falling with the swell, the two surfers were like tiny, weightless astronauts adrift in outer space. 'The sea,' says the poet Anne Stevenson, 'is as near as we come to another world.'

The following week, I was back on the Geelong freeway, the tyres sizzling across the rain-soaked bitumen. Far ahead in the distance, a wedge of cerulean sky hovered just above the horizon as if a door to that other world was slightly ajar. Very slowly, the patch of blue grew and the rain clouds rolled back until the sky was a promising collage of white and blue. As I pulled into the carpark at Jan Juc, I could feel my spirits lifting like steam from the road.

The surf was small and there was only one surfer out, but the swell was picking up with the incoming tide. With the wind blowing off the land, the waves were clean. Giant cumulus like puffed up tenors paraded overhead sending bursts of sunshine and shadow racing across the water. The other surfer and I happily shared what was on offer beneath this operatic sky. I had recently started doing yoga again, and instead of feeling out of form, I was conscious of a newly found looseness in my body as I moved across the waves. Although my wetsuit wasn't thick enough for near-winter conditions and I had no booties, I stayed out as long as I could, as long as I could tolerate my clattering teeth and vibrating bones. For once, I didn't mind pulling my clothes on over my damp, gritty skin. The warmth inside the car seeped through my arms and legs in a delicious hum, and as my body thawed, I felt preternaturally alert. Everything I laid eyes on, no matter how mundane, seemed fascinating. The concrete overpasses in Geelong took on the hyperreal vividness of a Jeffrey Smart painting. The You Yangs, which had always been a slouching blur in the distance to one side of the M1 freeway, now seemed suddenly close; close enough for me to make out individual trees on their flanks. And above it all loomed those high-stacked cumulus, so monumental it seemed a wonder they didn't fall from that operatic sky. I turned on the Eagles for the first time in months and sang my way home.

There was swell but not too much, the sun was out and the air so balmy it was hard to believe we were on the verge of winter. I gave Jack a call. He suggested that we go to Winkipop, the reef break at the northern end of Bells Beach which is almost as famous as Bells itself. From the cliff top, the view was so clear we could see the Heads, the Point Lonsdale lighthouse and the long sweep of the Peninsula all the way to Cape Schanck.

'You can imagine what it would be like in a big swell,' Jack said as we stood at the water's edge studying the shorebreak. The steeply slanting beach caused the incoming waves to suck back, rear up and smack the sand with uncommon ferocity. Jack was thinking of that Anzac Day twenty years ago when, half-drowned, he had been swept up here from Bells and had clawed his way up this patch of sand only to be dragged back time and again by the dumpers. He pointed up the beach to the spot where he had left his son Carl to play.

Catching sight of the bluebird tattooed on Jack's right foot, I remembered something else he had told me. *Every surfer has their drowning story. You'll have yours too.* He hadn't been trying to scare me: he wanted me to appreciate that if I was serious about surfing I had to face up to what it might entail. A drowning story was, after all, a survival story. It was about what might have happened but didn't. The story you told when you made it back. I didn't want to believe that I would ever have one to tell, although whenever I was held down a fraction longer than usual during a wipe-out, Jack's words would flash through my head and I would wonder if it was storytime.

We waited for a lull between the waves and then sprinted into the water, launching our boards and paddling hard for the rip. It didn't take long to get around the small headland to where the waves were peeling with geometric precision over the Winkipop reef. While Jack positioned himself deep inside the take-off point – the place where the waves are most likely to begin breaking, but also the place where you are most likely to get caught by the larger set – I paddled across to the far edge of the break where I could study the waves and familiarise myself with them. Reef breaks tend to produce waves that are more even, predictable and slower than beach breaks, and Winkipop is known for affording exceptionally long rides.

As I paddled for my first wave I could hear Jack hooting and urging me on. Everything felt right as I rose to my feet and slid down the wave's face, but on the bottom turn the board stalled and I was sucked into the belly of the wave. The next time, I made sure I angled myself across the face of the wave, avoiding the sudden plummet and sharp bottom turn. As with all classic Winkipop waves, there was a mesmerising, machine-like perfection in the way this one unfurled. At first, I managed to hover high near the lip where the wave was thin and at its most translucent. Never had I been so conscious of defying the laws of gravity, of doing something akin to flight. Having little confidence in my ability to manoeuvre on the wave, I felt like a child on a bike saying, 'Look, Ma! No hands,' while waiting for the inevitable crash. But it didn't come this time and I meandered happily along the increasingly hollow face, turned at the bottom, then drifted up and over the back of the wave when it seemed to have run its course, pleased to have made my exit before it collapsed and dragged me shorewards onto the rocks. Jack told me later that the wave had kept on peeling; I could have ridden it for another fifty metres or more. I didn't care. I'd got my taste of Winkipop's magic.

The cold water was now making itself felt, and I told Jack I wanted to get out as soon as I could catch another wave. Still feeling the after-effects of the flu, I knew it would be foolish to press my luck. In my late teens and early twenties I used to wear a summer-weight, full-length wetsuit all through the winter. I could remember the crunchy feel of the frozen dew on the sand dunes before an early morning, mid-winter surf. Now, when the water temperature dropped below 12 degrees, I quickly grew cold, even in a winter suit.

Jack caught a good long wave that deposited him on the rocky shore quite a distance from the steps. From the water, I watched him pick his way over the knobbly, biscuity boulders as the broken waves surged around his feet, and wished there was a less hazardous exit. This was the price you paid for surfing Winkipop. To get out the way we came

in would mean paddling back around the headland and contending with a shorebreak that was notorious for its reluctance
to part with anything in it clutches. Jack disappeared up the
cliff and then returned to the bottom step, waiting to take my
board while I cautiously clambered my way towards him, then
heaved myself up from the rocks.

As we climbed the steps to the carpark, we talked about the
need for upper-body strength and Jack asked me what other
exercise I did. I mentioned that I went running a few times a
week, and that I figured picking up a fifteen-kilogram toddler
umpteen times a day was a kind of work-out too. I was conscious that my body was starting to show signs of returning
to its old shape for the first time since I had given birth. The
extra flab was falling away, my flesh felt tight on my bones.
I was feeling more alert, more alive and more capable out in the
surf than I had twenty years ago.

'There's something else that helps, especially here at
Winkipop,' Jack added. 'A killer instinct.'

I shot him a quick glance. I knew what he was getting at,
knew I needed to be more assertive in the line-up. Jack made
no concessions for me in the water. If I was going to surf, I had
to stand up for myself. Even if we were the only two surfers
out, I had to earn my waves. He wanted me to harden up,
to learn how to hassle and jostle for position, how to claim a
wave for myself. Because if I didn't – if I went on expecting
the other surfers to be chivalrous and sharing – I'd only get
disillusioned and want to give up. Sure, in ideal conditions,
surfing was the antithesis of this kind of competitiveness. But

most of the time, the conditions were not ideal. Naively perhaps, I didn't see why a greater spirit of generosity still couldn't prevail. And there were times when it did, when strangers would offer encouragement and pull back from waves to give me a go; or, more commonly, when they would accept that everyone was entitled to 'a turn'. But in crowded conditions – especially at a very territorial break like Winkipop – the principles of self-interest and rugged individualism usually won out. The best and most aggressive surfers dominated the waves.

'I'll have to work on the killer instinct,' I smiled. It gave me a sinking feeling just thinking about it. 'What do you recommend?'

'That's easy. Think of all the rejection slips you've ever received.' Jack dropped his board on the grassy verge near his car and laughed to himself. 'Actually, if I did that I'd probably get so worked up I wouldn't be able to surf.'

Like any writer, Jack knew how wounding those perfunctory rebuffs could be. Both writing and surfing were, above all, mind games. There was no end to the struggle to keep up your confidence, to quell that rising panic, to keep believing that you had what it took. The constant pushing against your limitations, always asking yourself, *How far out of my depth can I go?* But as an ex-boxer, Jack also knew how to harness this insecurity and the sting of these knock-backs, how to draw on the fighter in himself, how to make the hurt and fear work for him. It made me wonder what had attracted him to boxing in the first place. I thought about the nuns at the boarding school where Jack had gone for a year – Sisters of Mercy who dished out regular beatings. When I suggested that this experience might have had something to do with it, Jack said he didn't think so. He put it down to Hemingway and to growing up in a prosperous suburb.

'I'd read almost everything that Hemingway wrote, and the characters in his stories were often bullfighters, soldiers or boxers, people whose lives had colour and intensity. I started boxing to pick up on some of that. The boxer knows that he stands alone and that his own courage and resources will be what carry him through. Where I grew up it was fairly genteel. People didn't think much of boxing. But I had a feeling it was part of a more authentic sort of life, and that it would quickly teach me things about myself.'

I realised that Jack had taken up boxing for the same reasons I'd taken up surfing – the search for something beyond the secure, insulated lives we'd known; the need to test our limits, to escape from what Robert Louis Stevenson calls the 'feather-bed of civilisation'. To feel the 'globe granite under-foot . . . strewn with cutting flints'. And central to that urge had been works of literature.

Jack's latest book, which was about veteran boxers, was about to be released. In my copy he wrote, 'From one fighter to another. Keep writing. Keep surfing.' But was I really a fighter in the sense Jack meant? I doubted it. One thing had become clear to me, something I hadn't wanted to face up to when I was younger. I was not and never would be a natural in the surf. In certain conditions I was reasonably capable but

I didn't have the fearlessness or natural talent that makes a good surfer. And I probably loved it all the more because I was so painfully aware of my shortcomings. I could never take the good moments for granted. When I was a girl I *was* quite a good netballer. Small and fast, I was often underestimated by my opponents, and I was good at capitalising on that. But I never won the Best and Fairest Award. What I won, year after year, was the Determination Award. I feared it would be my epitaph. *She was most determined.*

CHAPTER 4

Big Wave Hunting

WINTER

Colac

AUSTRALIA

VICTORIA

Lorne

Port Campbell

Broken
Head

Cape Otway

GREAT

OCEAN

ROAD

SOUTHERN

OCEAN

I HAD BEEN travelling the back roads from Colac for almost two hours when the ground began to rise like a grass-green wave. Suddenly, on the other side of the crest, farmland gave way to the sheer, honeycomb cliffs and there lay the deep blue wilderness of the Southern Ocean. While driving through the sleepy, dairy country of western Victoria where centuries of farming had tamed the land and recent rains had made it lush and slightly boggy, I had found it hard to believe that somewhere over the next hill or the next lay the explosive mass of the ocean, its fortress-like coastline home to some of the biggest surf in the country. Just off shore, the sandstone monoliths of the Twelve Apostles stood like marooned sentinels from prehistory. Not all of the Apostles were visible because of the indented cliffs, and I was conscious of the temptation to take my eyes off the dips and curves of the Great Ocean Road. For all their sublimity, their awesome size and scale, it was the Apostles' almost human appearance that distracted me. Stranded between sea and land, like the last of an ancient race, they seemed to occupy a tantalising interstice between animate and inanimate, civilisation and nature, past and present.

The road veered abruptly right into the small town of Port Campbell. With its lovely, deep harbour and small half-moon beach sheltered from the ocean by high cliffs on either side, it was a welcome refuge from the windy coast. The dramatic change of scenery brought with it a striking shift in aesthetics. After contending with a flamboyantly Romantic vista of the open ocean in violent collision with long stretches of sheer rock, here one was met by a neo-classical picture in which the sea was soothingly tranquil. Nature took on a human scale, appearing to conform to the rules of art. There was a protected cove, a wooden jetty on which a fisherman might sit to while away the hours, a beach on which young children could safely play. It was like stepping into a seaside idyll.

The surf break of Two Mile Bay, which gave Port Campbell its small measure of fame, lay to the west of this inlet. While Waimea Bay in Hawaii is known as *the* big wave destination against which all others are measured, Two Mile Bay is one of a small number of breaks around the world ranked just below Waimea. It is, however, a mercurial place. Most days, you would be lucky to see a wave there at all. Only when the swell reaches a critical mass, when it is over ten foot, will Two Mile explode into life. Within a few hours a relatively flat, untroubled ocean can rise with volcanic energy to a height of fifteen or twenty feet.

It wasn't until the late 1970s that anyone dared imagine riding these gigantic waves. One of the first to venture out was a surfer called Russell McConachy, whom I had come to see. He was standing in front of his harbourside rental apartment, one arm raised in greeting. In the 1950s, big wave surfing adopted a warrior ethos defined by displays of machismo and extraordinary risk-taking. With Hemingwayesque bravado, big wave surfers called their boards 'rhino-chasers' and 'elephant guns'. Russell had built his life around surfing the biggest waves the Southern Ocean could throw up and was known within the surfing community as 'Hellman' McConachy. Yet I knew from our telephone conversations that he was quietly spoken, level-headed and highly articulate. Not your average hellman. That he was driven was without doubt, but gung-ho or brazen he was not. Now as he shook my hand, it was hard not to wonder what demons lurked behind his mild smile.

It is generally agreed that ten feet and upwards constitutes a 'big wave'. Yet no wave can be reduced to a simple measurement, just as no measurement can do justice to all the elements that contribute to the ever-changing landscape which the surfer inhabits. Waves, after all, are not mountains, with crevices and footholds that can be clung to, explored, calibrated and made familiar. When you catch a wave and steady yourself by stretching out your hand to carve an arc in its liquid face, leaning your weight against it, nothing feels as solid and substantial as that moving wall of water. Yet a wave is not a thing at all but a fluid, rambunctious manifestation of energy, tantalisingly immaterial and thumpingly real. While waves can be measured empirically, each individual's perception of the surf is so utterly relative to ability, experience and temperament that the size of a wave is as much in the mind as in the sea. For me, any wave over five foot – taller than me – is big. For the average experienced surfer, a big wave might be eight foot and over. But 'big wave' surfers operate on a whole other scale that is almost impossible for the rest of us to comprehend.

The question 'How big?' and the current obsession with pushing the limits through the use of surf-skis to tow surfers onto waves of forty or fifty or sixty feet – waves which they would be unable to paddle into – did not really interest me. I wanted to fathom what drove a surfer to enter the realm of the big wave in the first place; I wanted to glimpse what entering that realm might feel like. And yet, with all the triumphalist talk in the surf media about conquering new frontiers, it was comforting to know there would always be waves that lay beyond man's grasp, that the biggest waves of all – invisible, undersea waves that break against the Gulf Stream and other strong currents – would never be ridden. These waves 'move on their mysterious courses far down in the hidden depths of the sea, rolling ponderously and unceasingly,' writes Rachel Carson in *The Sea Around Us*. They are waves 'such as never moved at the surface of the ocean' – water masses unthinkably great, some of them as high as three hundred feet.

With his wetsuit in his backpack and his board under one arm, Russell climbed nimbly down the cliff towards the beach followed by his girlfriend, Val Young. Dressed in a smart, vinyl coat and beret, she made an incongruously stylish sight on the crumbly red bluff. Val was the most knowledgeable non-surfer I had ever met. Before she met Russell she had had no interest in surfing, although she had always loved this part of the coast, having spent her childhood holidays near Peterborough. Five years of watching Russell in the water and a naturally curious mind had turned her into a sharp-eyed spectator and a canny commentator. She now derived great pleasure from watching the surf because she understood what she was seeing.

With flat water at Two Mile Bay, we had come to Bowkers, seventeen kilometres from Port Campbell, a beach break east of the Twelve Apostles. Val and I found a comfortable spot against some rocks at one end of the cuttlefish-strewn beach and watched as Russell paddled out through the shorebreak and into the solid six-foot waves beyond. This was not the big wave surfing I had anticipated but there was always the hope that the surf would pick up tomorrow.

Looking through Val's binoculars, I caught Russell's sinewy body in the circular frames as he slipped easily into a gnarly right-hander and scalloped his way across its face. He had a smooth, classical style as opposed to the fast cut and thrust favoured by younger, small wave surfers. Big waves do not allow for snappy manoeuvres, and Russell's style bore the hallmarks of his preference for more sizeable surf. Being fifty-two years old also meant that, like Jack, he didn't feel the need to tear up a wave to prove his prowess. He did worry, though, about the effect of ageing on his ability to handle bigger surf.

While his surfing had improved over the years, he had become more cautious, more prey to doubt, more selective about the waves he chose to ride. It was an inescapable part of growing older and he feared where it might lead.

That day at Bowkers there was no easily identifiable take-off point. Some waves were predictable and would peel nicely, others reared up tantalisingly only to curl into one long barrel and collapse in a rumbling heap of foam. But Russell was making it look easy.

'It still surprises me that he has no fear,' Val remarked. 'He doesn't have that natural apprehension that most people have. As the surf grows bigger, he gets more and more excited. The night before a big surf, he finds it hard to sleep. He's just like a kid, in that way. All that keenness, that passion.'

Val let out a characteristically throaty laugh. 'Sometimes, Russell will turn to me and say, "Wouldn't you rather be with someone younger?" I say to him, "How could I possibly be with someone younger than you?" In his attitude he hasn't left his twenties. Sometimes it's absolutely delightful and some-times it's so frustrating.'

Russell rarely bothered with the modest left-hander that broke just outside Port Campbell harbour but as I had expressed interest in trying it that afternoon, he said he'd come out too. I was getting a cold but having come all this way with my board, I felt I should make use of it. A good surf, I hoped, would clear my head (in fact, within days I would come down with a virus that would keep me out of the water for almost two months), and the two- to three-foot waves peeling off the point looked harmless enough.

It was worth paddling out just for the view of the coastline and the Twelve Apostles lit up by the sinking sun. Closest to us, only a few kilometres away, was the squat, rocky pillar of the Haystack with its distinctively thatched shape smouldering in the mellow, late afternoon light. Van Gogh could not have made it look more luminous and yet it also had a sinister quality, like a giant gravestone majestically indifferent to the events that swirled around it.

As usual, I sat to one side of the break for a time to study the waves and watch the other surfers. Conscious of being in strange waters, I knew I would not begin to feel comfortable until I had caught a wave. The reef, however, was clearly visible beneath the surface and I had never been comfortable with reef breaks. I decided to wait for a slightly larger set that would break further out into the channel, away from the rocks. When an inviting wave loomed, I paddled into it and leapt to my feet but didn't manage to angle the board sharply enough to travel across the peeling, deep green face. Instead of moving parallel with the shore across the unbroken wave, I found myself riding the whitewater straight towards the cliff. By the time I had dived off the board, it was too late. I was being washed over the rocks not far from the base of the cliff. The surf wasn't large and the broken waves were not hitting the reef with anything like life-threatening ferocity, but the water was relatively shallow and I could feel the reef beneath me as I half stumbled, half swam through the buffeting waves.

More than being afraid, I was mortified that I'd been inept enough to let this happen. A few of the other surfers were looking in my direction, clearly wondering if I was all right. At the edge of my vision I could see the Haystack silently reminding me of my folly and of how quickly things could go wrong. I scanned the base of the nearby cliff, searching for a patch of sand or a ledge I might scramble onto if necessary. I had seen a surfer launch himself from the cliff rather than paddle out from the pier, and wondered if I could clamber to shore that way; but it looked too difficult. Instead, I waited for a lull in the waves and managed to paddle back into the deep channel.

A passing surfer asked if I'd copped many holes from the reef. 'It happens to all of us,' he said.

'I'm okay,' I said, forcing a smile. In the fading light, I watched the local surfers, Russell among them, whipping in and out of the waves as if there was nothing to it, as if it was the easiest thing in the world. Much as I wanted to catch another wave to show myself (and the other surfers) that I hadn't lost my nerve, I couldn't do it. Each time a promising wave loomed, I would begin to paddle only to pull back at the last moment, frozen by the thought of ending up on the rocks again. My bones were rattling with cold and I knew there was no point persisting. As a violet haze settled over the water, I began the long paddle back to the beach.

Russell's church-like, bluestone house, with its massive beams from the Geelong woolstore, salvaged leadlight fittings and lofty, bush-framed view of Two Mile Bay, was a world away from the tough, bayside suburb of Chelsea where he had grown up, a street-fighter in neighbourhood gangs. His love affair with Two Mile began in 1979 when he first saw it breaking in all its splendour. Very few people had surfed those waves, and when Russell got out there he understood why: they were thicker and huger than anything he had ever known. To inhabit them was to step into another dimension.

Russell ran his insurance business from Torquay but spent as much time as he could in Port Campbell. When the storms he had been tracking from Africa delivered the kind of swell that kept most surfers on dry land, he dropped all engagements and was transformed from a mild-mannered insurance agent into a man possessed. His surfing diary, which recorded every encounter he had ever had with waves at Two Mile, was not just an aid to memory or a record of achievement but a way of giving shape to his life, a way of mapping the shifting topography of Two Mile and consolidating his knowledge of every nook and cranny of its coastline. Put together, these entries formed a narrative of obsession with a place and with a way of being *in extremis*. In the early days, he hadn't recorded any wave as being over fifteen foot, because he couldn't believe it was possible that they might be bigger. True big waves were mythical creatures that fetched up in places like Hawaii; they didn't happen in his own backyard. Only gradually did he begin to realise that the waves he was surfing at Two Mile could rival those he had seen in footage of Waimea Bay.

The same impulse that drove Russell to keep his journal had also driven him to return obsessively to a cathedral-sized cave between Two Mile Bay and the Port Campbell harbour. It had almost claimed his life. If death had taken on any shape for Russell over the years, it had acquired the features of this cave, which had become the shadowy 'other' of the cavernous waves he willingly entered.

It happened on an overcast day in the mid-1990s, with the swell peaking at a towering twenty feet. Russell and two friends, Steve and Rock, were the only surfers who dared to go out. As the sky darkened, so did the water and the silver-grey clouds could be seen reflected in the massive faces of the waves. With each successive wave, Russell grew more confident, felt himself pushing through mental barriers that had previously held him back. He edged deeper and deeper inside the take-off zone to better position himself. All surfers know that finding the wave's G-spot is a trade-off, a calculated risk: the deeper you go, the greater the danger of being swamped by a bigger set breaking further out. But in big wave surfing the stakes are astronomically high. Russell had been surfing for three hours when the odds went against him and a bigger set steamed through, catching him out. With a wave about to collapse on top of him, he bailed off his board and dived for the bottom. As the wave held him down 'in the black', the extraordinary pressure rolling above him stretched his leg rope until it snapped, inflicting a psychological blow as well as a physical one. His leg rope was his umbilical cord, his connection to the world above the surface. Now it was gone.

When he surfaced, bomboras were breaking all the way up the coast. He should have headed for the main channel of Port Campbell harbour; instead, he chose to swim in search of his board. Soon he was being pushed by ten-foot-high avalanches of whitewater towards a large cave. Duck-diving endlessly under each wall of foam to escape its turbulence, he knew he was close to spinning out of control. There was no time for fear, no time to feel anything at all: he had to swim for his life. Through a combination of superb fitness, local knowledge and good luck, he managed to get beyond the cave and around the next point, where his mates were waiting for him.

As soon as he was out of the water, Russell returned to the clifftop above the cave and sat staring out to sea, watching the waves and trying to digest what had happened. An hour later, he had just started walking away when something made him look back: a fragment of his board was floating out of the cave like a vision of the fate he had narrowly escaped.

Since then, whenever he went surfing at Two Mile, Russell was conscious of the cave lurking in wait for him. When the ocean was flat, he would sometimes paddle into the cave, climb onto a shelf and sit thinking about what he would do if he were to be washed in there.

To explore the contours of death, as Russell explored the contours of his cave, was clearly a powerful driving force for those attracted to extreme, death-defying activities. It was the dream of visiting the underworld without becoming one of its captives. Freud contends that civilisation has evolved out of the struggle between Eros and Death, between the instinct for life and the instinct for destruction. As in other arenas of controlled aggression such as boxing or martial arts, big wave surfing puts that primal struggle on spectacular display. In most of us the conflict is all but invisible: our aggressive instincts are turned inwards, in the formation of the superego. Thou shalt, thou shalt not, commands the superego, directing and controlling our desires. But for those driven to turn their aggressive instincts outwards, to give vent to the forbidden destructive impulse, defiance of the superego's interdictions can yield the most intense of 'narcissistic' satisfactions: the fulfilment of the ego's yearning for omnipotence.

We were standing on the high cliff top above the cave when Russell told me his 'drowning story' and the obsession it had spawned. The ocean in front of us was dead flat, although it now exuded a palpable air of menace.

'Next time you're here,' he promised, 'you'll see what I mean.'

The depths of winter had finally passed and there was more than a touch of spring in the air. For months there had been no swell. The waves at Jan Juc were intermittent and very small, but I was so hungry for a surf I was grateful for anything that could be ridden. As the tide dropped, there were more snappy, translucent waves to be caught, good practice for quickly angling the board across the face before it disappeared. In such conditions, there was not the slightest touch of menace in the water, not even the occasional frisson of danger. It was good therapy after my loss of nerve at Port Campbell, although the memory of it would continue to haunt me whenever I found myself surfing over the dark shapes and boils of a reef. I stayed in the gold-threaded water for two and a half hours and had to force myself to get out. I wanted to stay there forever and live on a wave.

I had never had the slightest desire to seek out the monstrous Southern Ocean waves that Russell lived for, and so it always came as a shock to remember that I had surfed them – in a ship.

It was late 1987. I was twenty-five and about to resign my job as a journalist to go to Europe when the editor called me into his office. The paper needed a correspondent for the final leg of the First Fleet Re-Enactment, a showpiece event of the Bicentennial celebrations. It would mean flying to Fremantle and boarding a square-rigged tall ship to sail through the Great Australian Bight and up the south-eastern coast to Sydney. As he talked about the assignment and how there were plenty in the newsroom who would give their eye-teeth to do it, I felt a queasiness like the first twinges of seasickness. I was flattered to be asked, but the thought of being trapped on an antique boat for four weeks in the Southern and Pacific oceans with a bunch of strangers was not my idea of adventure. Give it to one of the others, I longed to say. I had never been one for messing about in boats or for the open ocean. It was the littoral that I loved, the edge of things, the in-between zone where land and water overlapped.

The choice was mine, of course, my editor told me. But in reality, there was no choice. If I didn't take up his offer, I knew I would always wonder what I had missed out on; would always regret my lack of courage.

Four weeks later I was clutching the rails of the flagship of the fleet, the *Søren Larsen*, heading for Cape Leeuwin. The horizon sank and re-appeared behind the waves. Engine fumes churned in the air as we motored against the wind. The coast was long gone, and the whole ship was braced and fighting the sea. I went down below and lay on my coffin-sized bunk, shifting my toes to avoid a steady drip fed by every wave that washed the deck. There was nothing soothing about this heaving; never a moment's stillness or silence as the ship rocked and pitched. The wooden boards creaked and the rigging whined. Whenever I tried to get up, I threw up.

It went on for two days. By the third, I was able to sit on deck with some of the other new crew members who were also finding their sea legs and we managed to laugh. The sky was cloudless. That afternoon the engine was turned off and we started sailing at a gentle three knots. The *Bounty* appeared in the distance like a grey ghost ship, and sailed close enough for us to greet those on board before it disappeared again over the edge of the world. The ships in the fleet had scattered on the first day and none, apart from the *Bounty*, had been sighted since.

As sailors do, I was discovering how little ships in big waves concentrate the mind. How, in the early stages of a voyage as brain and body adapt, the sea acts as a buffer between the self and thoughts of civilisation. It was hard to even contemplate what those on land might be doing. Our square-rigged, wooden-hulled sailing ship and its small community had become the moving centre of the world.

We had radios for communication and an engine if we lacked wind but few other advantages over the original fleet. The coast might be known this time around, the country colonised, but the route between Fremantle and Sydney remained as unpredictable as it had been two hundred years before. Never had Australia's early history felt so threateningly immediate. Although the captains of the nine ships wanted to follow the original route south around the southern tip of Tasmania, the commodore of the fleet had decided that they would sail through Bass Strait instead in order to reach Jervis Bay by the middle of January. It was expected that this route would mean adverse winds, because of the easterlies that prevailed at this time of the year, and the captains were not impressed by the prospect of motoring much of the distance in order to meet the schedule.

In a way, I could appreciate their frustrations, although mine were of a very different order. When I went surfing I was captain of my craft and could largely dictate the terms of my engagement with the ocean. The temporary abandon of surfing was exhilarating because I could decide when I'd had enough and head for the shore. But here, my fate was out of my hands and there was no avenue of escape. No getting away from the other forty-two people on board, no getting away from the uncertainty of what lay ahead. Clearly I was too fond of being in control of my environment; I loved the sea but did not trust it.

At night, the rolling was often so violent that I would lie rigid in my bunk, half believing that if I stopped willing the ship to right itself we would go down. When the engine was off and the sails up, the ship rolled from side to side rather than front to back. But instead of letting this more pleasant rocking motion lull me to sleep, I kept jolting myself awake, ready to rush on deck if the alarm was sounded. I felt safest there, where I could see what was going on.

The importance of muster drill had been impressed upon us with the story of the square-rigger the *Marques*, which sank in a matter of minutes after being swamped by a freak wave off the coast of Bermuda in the early 1980s, its lights still burning as it disappeared beneath the water. The image haunted me for the rest of the trip. I took to standing at the helm behind the wheelhouse. If we were going to be swamped, I wanted to be the first to know. With a big sea running, great surges of water, the likes of which I had only ever seen in disaster movies, curled menacingly over the stern of the 145-foot ship and made the horizon look vertical. As we surfed down these massive slopes, our bow almost disappeared in each trough. The captain was positively gleeful. But it was not my idea of surfing.

On the night of my first watch, the sandy-haired second bosun sang a sea-shanty as the ominous fuzz of a Force Nine gale advanced from the west. To distract us from the weather, he told stories about earlier legs of the voyage. There had been an albatross caught on the lure of a fishing line which, when freed, stayed for three days, walking around the deck, bending with the motion of the ship like an experienced sailor. One night when Edward Coleridge, the great-great-great-great nephew of Samuel Taylor, was on board, 'The Rime of the Ancient Mariner' was read aloud on deck. Another time, the ship came upon whales feeding upon miles of tiny krill that had turned the sea the colour of blood. The one story never told, however, was that of Hendrik Nielsen, first mate on the *Anna Kristina*, who was lost overboard en route to Cape Town.

Why do I think of you, dead man? On night watch, especially when the seas were high, it was impossible not to think of death. Sitting at the bowsprit watching the moon rise, I found my way inside Kenneth Slessor's 'Five Bells' like a genie slipping into a bottle. It was a poem I had loved for its sinuous, watery language, for its waves with 'diamond quills and combs of light / That arched their mackerel-backs and smacked the sand / In the moon's drench'. I had admired it as an artefact but had, until now, been tone-deaf to its tolling music. As the ship's bell divided up the hours, I thought of Hendrik Nielsen, whom I had never met, and of Joe, 'long dead, who lives between five bells'. Joe, who no longer rides the waves but is ridden by them. I was only twenty-five, and death was still something that happened to other people. Even so, my fear of what might befall the ship was real. To lose control over your fate, however temporarily, is to begin to understand the tenuous nature of your grasp on life.

But when the sea was calm and the stars hung in the water and tiny, phosphorescent creatures sparkled in the ship's wake and a mandarin moon beckoned, fear gave way to wonder:

> There moved the multitudinous stars,
> and coloured birds and fishes moved.
> There swam the sliding continents.
> All time lay rolled in me, and sense,
> and love that knew not its beloved.

Murmuring Judith Wright's 'Woman to Child' to the night air, I did not give much thought to the maternal symbolism of the ocean. Like death, giving birth was also something that happened to other people. Wright's song seemed as much a hymn to her creative powers as it was to her unborn child. Night watch did not inspire in me the kind of 'motherhood longings' it stirred in Dora Birtles when she was sailing the Arafura Sea. For Birtles, who wrote about her experience in *North-West by North*, the heaving ocean became 'the All-Mother, the watery womb that produced the first life'.

> . . . a petrel kept flying round and round in circles
> over my head and over the wake stretched like a
> galloping mare's tail behind the boat. The bird was so
> black against the moon. I thought that had my dream
> desires been fulfilled, I had read them as motherhood

longings, it might be a disembodied spirit trying to get a lodgment within me. That conviction grew as the bird kept on weaving the rings of its flight about me. Finally it perched near the end of the boom not a yard from me. Its tail folded looked like a pair of scissors half-open. It made no sound, its beak pointing as if it would pierce my breast. Fascinated I let the ship get off the course a little and was aware of a wave bigger than any that night, immediately astern, coming sideways with a hissing indrawn breath and a curl of white on its forehead. So I had to nurse the boat over that and over two more big ones and when I looked again the bird had gone.

I was a decade away from knowing 'motherhood longings', but on those calmer nights, as I meditated on the waves rolling beneath us, I finally stopped resisting the endless rocking and gave myself up to the forces beyond my control. There were even brief occasions when I felt secure and almost serene, when it seemed we were floating inside a globe rather than sailing across one.

Two weeks after leaving Fremantle, we sighted Cape Otway on the port bow and King Island to starboard. We were entering Bass Strait. Once we rounded Cape Otway we were protected from the full force of the Southern Ocean swells but Bass Strait was not to be underestimated. Here, as the Melbourne writer Stephen Murray-Smith observes, 'A placid, easy sea, no more than a little "jobbley", as I've heard it called, can become a monstrous thing, great waves splintering themselves against granite rocks and islands and a screaming wind obliterating with drift the sea and the land and the sky itself.' No one who has been caught by a sudden change on Bass Strait, he writes, 'will ever deny there's a lot of sea there'.

The strait was eerily calm at first and the bright sunshine made all the talk of its dangers seem overwrought. Having been spurred on by furious winds and swell in the Southern Ocean, we were now ahead of schedule and had time to stop for a swim. Later, when the wind picked up a little and we were able to sail, a school of dolphins joined us like a welcoming party, surfing in group formation the waves displaced by the ship. The joyous show lasted half an hour and suddenly they were gone.

Two days later we were having our evening meal when one of the watch-crew scrambled down the gangway: a storm was approaching. Abandoning the table, we pulled on our wet-weather gear and went on deck. My heart sank as I stood watching what was coming our way. It looked like a scene out of a child's picture book, where puffy-cheeked, black clouds with angry faces spout gale-force winds from puckered mouths. Ragged blades of lightning knifed the sky, followed by Wagnerian rumblings. It was the most riotous cosmic display I had ever witnessed but I was in no position to relish it. All was wet, roaring confusion as we lurched drunkenly across the deck, tackling the mainsail ropes to set the storm sail. Furtively I scanned the faces of the permanent crew, their hair dripping with rain and spray, for signs of reassurance amid the chaos. As the wind strengthened, the ship's bell rang of its own volition, filling the air with wild, erratic clangs. We were lucky that the seas had been flat earlier in the day. What it would have been like if the storm had hit when we were surfing the giant swells of the Southern Ocean didn't bear thinking about.

The next morning, the sun streamed in golden columns through the open hatches of the saloon and the ocean sparkled as if it had been polished by the raging winds of the previous night. The following day we arrived at Eden, our first landfall since Fremantle.

Landfall at Eden after the dark night of the soul. Thirteen years later, as I read back over my journal, my account of our arrival at Eden had a disturbingly self-satisfied ring. The public mood in Australia was now far removed from that of the Bicentennial year. Although the arrival of the First Fleet in Sydney Harbour had not been without controversy – after all, it was hardly a reason for celebration for the Aboriginal population – many Australians had revelled in the sight of so many boats, many full of foreigners, thronging the water. Now, in 2001, the image of boats arriving on our shores had taken on a totally different meaning; had acquired an almost hallucinatory quality as a bitter, divisive debate about asylum-seekers continued to rage. There were those who believed the boats should be turned around, or towed away or even shot at. Later in the year, desperate people in sinking boats would be falsely accused by the government of throwing their children overboard. Above all, the official message was that 'these people' were not like 'us'. Oceania might never have been the paradise hailed by Cook and Bougainville, but these days it was looking closer to the Oceania of George Orwell's *Nineteen Eighty-Four*. In this nightmarish world, Oceania – comprising the Americas, the British Isles, Australasia and the southern portion of Africa – is one of three great superstates, along with Eurasia and Eastasia, all of which are constantly at war with each other. One day Winston Smith, Orwell's hero, writes in a diary about the war flicks he has seen the night before.

One very good one of a ship full of refugees
being bombed somewhere in the Mediterranean.
Audience much amused by shots of a great huge
fat man trying to swim away with a helicopter
after him . . . then you saw lifeboat full of children
with a helicopter hovering over it. There was a
middle-aged woman might have been a jewess
sitting up in the bow with a little boy about three
years old in her arms. Little boy screaming with
fright and hiding his head between her breasts as
if he was trying to burrow right into her and the
woman putting her arms around him and comforting
him although she was blue with fright herself,
all the time covering him up as much as possible
as if she thought her arms could keep the bullets
off him.

Like all satire, *Nineteen Eighty-Four* takes callousness to an extreme to make its point; yet Orwell's scenario was not so distant from some of the 'solutions' to the boat-people's situation proposed on Australian talk-back radio.

I had begun my re-enactment journal with a quotation from the historian Paul Carter's *The Road to Botany Bay* about the making of Australian history after the arrival of the First Fleet. It concludes, 'The sea, formerly asylum, itself becomes a prison, a turbulent, unavoidable barrier to progress.' How eerily appropriate this observation now sounded thirteen years on. The sea, which promised asylum, *had* become a prison for those adrift with nowhere to go. And our progress as a society *was* being retarded by our desire for the ocean to remain not just a barrier but a fortress.

CHAPTER 5

The Pacific Solution

SPRING

*Civilisation is terrible, but don't
imagine that you can ever escape it.*

Iris Murdoch, THE SEA, THE SEA

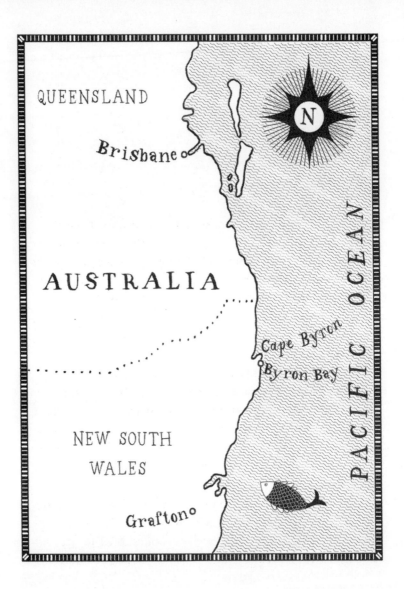

THE SKY HAD that watermelon glow it gets just before sunrise as my sister, Melinda, and I climbed into a taxi which took us to the airport. I was grateful that my son was still asleep as I had been too cowardly to tell him I was going. The take-off felt like a physical wrench and I gazed miserably out the window until, in what seemed like no time, we were flying over Cape Byron, looking down on the Pacific from ten thousand feet.

Melinda and I had last been in Byron Bay together in late February 1982. Melinda, an art student, had been attracted by the creative experiments in alternative living, the legacy of the hippie movement, for which the Byron region was famous. I had come for the surf. We were both, in our different ways, trying to escape the insular suburban world in which we had grown up. In the disco-driven late 1970s, it was Melinda who had introduced me to the country and West Coast rock of the hippie era: the Eagles, Jackson Browne, Neil Young, Van Morrison, the Moody Blues and the soundtrack to the cult surfing movie *Morning of the Earth*. It might have been the

Age of Disco but for those of us who still identified with the Age of Aquarius, Byron Bay was a spiritual home.

We took the *Spirit of Progress* to Sydney and then an old red rattler. Each time we parted with our luggage, I watched with horror as my first surfboard – a second-hand single fin wrapped in an old sheet – was unceremoniously tossed into the guard's van. Two sleepless nights later, we staggered out of the train and into what felt like another country. The air was saturated, and after Melbourne, where nature is confined to public parks, the vegetation here was so rampant and spectacular as to be almost overwhelming. Byron was yet to be discovered by mainstream tourism, and the town was still sleepy and serene. Stepping gingerly over the squashed cane toads on the footpath, we passed kombi vans full of ragged-haired surfers munching lentil burgers, women in swirling batik skirts, and clothes shops wafting patchouli oil. It was indeed another world.

Twenty years on, Byron Bay was no longer a sleepy country town. The most obvious change was the permanent traffic-jam in the main street. Although the township was much bigger and a little glossier, it had wisely capitalised on what made it distinctive: surfing, alternative therapies, backpacker hostels and ecologically oriented tourism were all thriving industries. Somehow, the mellow ambience and relaxed mood had managed to survive. Passing a newsagent, we picked up a copy of the independently owned local paper, the *Byron Shire Echo*, to find that it contained five pages of fiercely articulate letters, mostly about the local council's decision to downgrade the Arakwal National Park to a regional park. Beneath the trappings of New

Age entrepreneurialism, the political and social consciousness of the hippie era lived on in community activism and resistance to development. The results were plain to see. No high-rise hotels, garish golden arches or the large-scale resorts like Club Med that were a feature of so many coastal resorts.

For the Aboriginal community, however, paradise had long been lost. In the *Echo*, a custodian of the Arakwal tribe, Lorna Kelly, spoke of the changes she had witnessed over fifty years. 'I've seen the whole of Byron Bay being taken away piece by piece and developed, and our special places destroyed in the process. Like the midden at The Pass where they built a boat ramp, the lighthouse where my grandfather went for men's business, Taylor's Lake, our women's area, destroyed by pollution and disrespect. Even the Wheel Resort is built on my grandfather's and grandmother's graves.'

I had fantasised about going back to Byron ever since taking up surfing again. Byron was special for many reasons, but in my private surfing mythos it had acquired the status of a sacred site. The home of my first 'real wave', it was the place where the idea of surfing had become a reality for me. Now, as the rest of the country closed in on itself like a clenched fist, Byron loomed like a paradisiacal enclave of goodwill.

The prevous month, over four hundred refugees had been plucked from their sinking boat by a Norwegian container vessel, the *Tampa*, one hundred and forty kilometres from

Christmas Island. To ensure that none of the boat people set foot on Australian soil, the government had responded with the 'Pacific solution': funding various small Pacific islands to detain the refugees until their claims for resettlement were addressed. To watch our political leaders go to these extraordinary lengths to avoid offering sanctuary to a boat-load of traumatised people, and to realise that they had wide public support, was to begin to understand what it might mean to become an exile in one's own land.

The beauty of Byron Bay was that it was full of exiles. In the late 1960s, the Byron region began to be transformed by a dramatic influx of newcomers from the cities and from all over the world who dreamed of building communities based on co-operation rather than competition. Although the shire was best known as the home of the back-to-earth communes, the first counterculture refugees in Byron were surfers. Nomadic and often poor, they tended to camp illegally on the beaches, moving on when pressed by the authorities. Many of these surfers had been politicised by the Vietnam War protest movement and were disillusioned with the emergence of surfing as a profession and commercial sport. Inspired by the hippie movement and disenchanted with the emphasis on competition, 'soul surfing', as it became known, found expression in surfing movies like *Morning of the Earth* in which a small group of surfers shun mainstream life for a more elemental existence – camping by the beach, smoking dope and riding perfect waves.

The first hippies who settled in the Byron hinterland

arrived not long after the surfers. They lived like reclusive hill tribes and were appalled when they heard that the Australian Union of Students planned to host their Aquarius Festival – Australia's answer to Woodstock – on a nearby property in 1973. It was this festival, eventually held at Nimbin, thirty kilometres inland from Byron, that brought in a flood of idealistic dropouts in search of a more community-minded, nonmaterialistic way life at one with nature. Their presence slowly transformed this traditionally conservative, rural region into the environmentally conscious, politically active and libertarian-minded enclave it had become.

The surfers and hippies who fled the cities for Byron Bay were classic examples of Freud's 'discontents'. They believed that civilisation was largely responsible for our misery and that, as Freud dryly summarised it, 'we should be much happier if we gave it up and returned to primitive conditions'. Freud himself was too much of an anti-utopian and too aware of the power of man's aggressive instincts to have much faith in such self-regulating social experiments; he believed that civilisation was the only way we could keep our fundamental aggressiveness in check. At the same time, he was fully aware of the escalating tension between Eros – the force prized by the hippies ('All you need is love') – and aggression – the force driving development and technology. In 1930, as fascism began to stir in Germany, he wrote: 'Men have gained control over the forces of nature to such an extent that with their help they would have no difficulty in exterminating one another to the last man. They know this, and hence comes a large part of their current unrest, their unhappiness and their mood of anxiety.'

In *The Book of Waves* Drew Kampion echoes the holistic philosophy of the hippie era in his paean to the wave. 'Everything is waves. The universe of space and matter is charged with energy, and this energy is organised by God or by forces far greater than ourselves into the pulsations we call waves. Waves of energy. Like echoes of the heartbeat of the absolute being, waves give expression to the divine will. They give form to the universe.' While I liked to think of myself as a child of soul surfing, I could not honestly share that kind of cosmology or its legacy in New Age spirituality. Not inclined to mysticism, I was struggling towards a way of thinking about the ocean that did not resort to the metaphysical. On the best days in the surf I understood the meaning of 'a peace that passeth all understanding', a peace born of reconnecting with the natural world after the daily alienation of life in the city, and experienced a sweet, fleeting sense of returning 'home'. I understood too what it might mean to feel part of a natural force infinitely greater than myself. But much as I was stirred by Romantic pantheism, my understanding of 'the oceanic feeling' was more biological and psychological than spiritual. While there was something deeply comforting about the idea of a unifying spirit that 'rolls through all things', as Wordsworth wrote, I could not claim to have known it.

In the days that followed the September 11 terrorist attacks in New York, as frenzied commentators in the Australian media began talking about civilisation versus barbarism, good versus evil, public alarm about the boat people as potential terrorists hardened into outright hostility. I could no longer bring myself to read the newspapers. All I wanted to do was head down to the coast, turn my back on 'civilisation' and paddle out to sea. It was at times like this that surfing came into its own as an antidote to the high-voltage horror of global events that were far beyond one's control. I craved space in which to gather my thoughts, to make sense of all that had happened.

Within an hour of arriving in Byron, Melinda and I were back at the main beach, blinking at the frosty white sand as if we had just emerged from a dark room. Straight ahead of us the blue Pacific rocked gently in the cradle of the bay. The sensation of being transported to another world was as strong this time as it had been on our first visit, and we happily gave ourselves up to it. I hired a board and frolicked in the small, clean waves while drinking in the view from the water – the conical shapes of the mountains beyond Mullumbimby, the sweep of the bay from Brunswick Heads in the north to the emerald rainforest of Cape Byron. Beneath the headland, a narrow neck of rocks plunged into the sea to form the Pass. I surfed wearing only my bathers, relishing the feel of the sun on my bare arms and legs; it was the first time I had gone without a wetsuit since my return to surfing. I had slept only fitfully the night before, anxious about the early start and about leaving my son. Now, as I paddled into the hollow little waves, I was wide awake, alert and full of energy. Everything, I reflected, had unfolded with such remarkable ease. I had grown so used to surfing being a major expedition and a test of nerve and determination that I had almost forgotten how simple, effortless and pleasurable it could be.

Sunning ourselves on the beach, Melinda and I laughed as we remembered our first day here twenty years ago. The gently fizzing surf had looked like child's play compared to Portsea and I had plunged in without a second thought. Melinda lazed on the beach, drifting in and out of sleep. After a time she stirred, sat up and scanned the water and, finally, spotted me. Puzzled as to what I was doing so far out, she waved; I waved back as though everything was fine. In fact, having swum out beyond the break, I had found myself in the grip of a powerful littoral current unlike anything I had experienced. Most rips travel perpendicular to the shore and I knew how to handle them, but this one ran parallel to it. In the small, fitful surf, I couldn't seem to find a wave strong enough to carry me shorewards. I had been awarded a surf lifesaving bronze at Portsea only a few months before and, although I doubted that I could save anyone else, I had grown more confident about my ability to save myself. Now here I was, a qualified lifesaver, struggling to extract myself from the mildest of Pacific swells. To halt my northward drift I grabbed onto a shell-encrusted pylon, one of the last remnants of the old meatworks jetty, and pondered what to do. A surfer paddled past and asked if I was all right. I tried to appear nonchalant, as though I was merely taking a breather, but I was deeply ashamed. After what felt like an age, I finally managed to catch a wave in to the shore.

Since buying my first board the year before, my encounters with the surf had been infrequent. Not having a car or surfing companions meant that just getting to the beach with my board had been a major enterprise. The waves I had caught so far did not qualify as what I thought of as 'real' surf: most were broken or half-broken, and afforded only the bumpiest of rides in the whitewater. How you managed to launch yourself into, let alone glide across, the glittering blue face of a proper, peeling wave was still a mystery to me. Every time I tried to paddle for an unbroken peak, I either failed to catch it or went somersaulting into the belly of a dumper.

But at our youth hostel in Byron, someone told me that the Wreck, just north of where I had been swimming, was a good surfing spot for beginners. The waves were just my size, the water like a warm bath. When you have spent your life swimming in the heavy-duty, Antarctic waters of Bass Strait, the Pacific comes as a revelation. Here on the easternmost tip of the continent, the brooding savagery of the Southern Ocean is forgotten. Rather than the sombreness engendered by looking downwards to the Pole, one is conscious of a lightness of mood, a dreamy expansiveness that comes of looking outwards to the world.

A wave came my way from some distant, tropical latitude, a glaucous, surging peak that did not lurch up violently and pitch me into freefall as so many frigid, southern waves had done, but swelled slowly, almost languidly, offering up its naked, rounded shoulder in an irresistible come-on. The shoulder curved into a gentle slope upon which my board found easy purchase, and leaping to my feet I made a dreamy, delighted descent. Archimedes could not have been happier when he leapt from his bath and cried *Eureka!* I had found – so it seemed at that moment – the answer to the mystery of how to walk on water. Many years later, while writing the early surfing scenes of *Night Surfing*, I would experience a similar thrill of discovery. *So this is how it is done!* It was not so much a moment of truth as a feeling of rightness and ease; of finally arriving at a place I had long been searching for, a place where I belonged.

Now, twenty years on, Melinda and I stood on the main beach, the fine white sand squeaking beneath our feet as we contemplated how different our lives might be if we could start each day this way. At this pristine hour, the sea was glycerine, disturbed only by rapid surges of energy near the shore. I grabbed my board and joined the two local surfers in the water. We shared the small, translucent waves and occasionally talked. When I told them where I was from, the younger, boyish-faced surfer said that he was thinking of heading south. I looked at him incredulously and was about to say, 'Why on earth would you want to leave all this?' when he asked if there was much work to be had in Melbourne or on the Victorian coast. Paradise is, of course, relative to one's prospects and one's state of mind, and the unemployment rate in the Byron region was among the highest in Australia.

'Surfers are always cynical about people who make money out of surfing 'cause they believe that simony is a sin.'

'Simony?'

'You know, like selling land in Hawaii. Profiting from sacred things.'

Rusty Miller was sitting at a busy outdoor cafe in the main street, his sinewy, weather-beaten frame hunched over a rickety wooden table. He was talking about how, after winning the United States Surfing Championship in 1964, he became one of the first surfers to make money out of the sport. Ambivalence about the commercialisation of surfing was a luxury he could not afford; commercialistion had allowed him to make a living from what he loved doing. Part of his income was still derived from giving private lessons in the traditional Hawaiian-style of surfing he had been taught as a boy in California. Rather than emphasising the aggressive, gymnastic manoeuvres that dominate modern surfing, Rusty stressed grace and poise, and the importance of riding the wave all the way to the shore.

Earlier that morning I'd had a lesson with him at Tallow Beach, the only break protected from the howling northerly wind. The main beach, Clark's Beach and the Pass were utterly windswept that day, but at Tallow, in the lee of Cape Byron, some reasonably clean little waves were rolling in.

After watching me catch a few, Rusty paddled over. 'It's obvious you're from the city.'

'What do you mean?' I asked.

'You're in such a hurry. You jump up too fast.' The transition from prone to standing should be more fluid, he said, demonstrating what he meant. 'Drag the side of your left foot across the surface of the board so that it's all one movement.'

I tried it a few times but found it hard to keep my balance when moving in what felt like slow motion. I was reminded of when I used to play the piano. I could often play pieces *allegro* with some panache, but as soon as I tried to play them more slowly, everything fell apart and it became apparent how little technical control I had. It was the same when I played tennis: I always seemed to be serving either aces or double faults.

At the cafe, we were talking about the changes in the Byron region since Rusty first came here in 1971, a refugee from the Nixon era who opposed the Vietnam War. 'It's not dropoutsville any more,' he said. 'If you wanta live here you better not come with less than two hundred and fifty grand. The whole surf-sand-sun thing is pretty much a production line now. A real barometer of what's happening is that you can never find a place to park. We've always fought against development but the persistent developers have got their way.' As a result, coastal erosion and sewage seeping into local rivers and creeks were serious problems.

Not long after Rusty came to Australia, he met the film-maker Albert Falzon. Along with a young surfer called Steven Cooney, they travelled to Bali and featured in footage for *Morning of the Earth*, now regarded as a surfing classic. With its psychedelic, slow-motion waves that seem to exist in an eternal dawn, shimmering green coast and occasional glimpses of Indonesian village life, the film conjures up an idyllic world remote from the pressures of urban existence. As fluid as the element it documents, it has no narrative: just sequence after sequence of mesmerising shots of surfers swooping through gilded barrels of water in Indonesia, Australia and Hawaii, accompanied by a soundtrack of songs with a cosmic bent.

Believing that evil spirits and demons lived in the ocean, the Balinese had no surfing tradition. While individual Western surfers had found their way to Bali from the 1930s onwards, surfing did not make an impact on the island until the late 1960s, when Australian surfers started venturing there. What has now become one of the most prized surfing locations in the world – Uluwatu on the Bukit Peninsula – was 'discovered' during the filming of *Morning of the Earth*. Word spread quickly about the new 'surfing paradise' and a tourism boom followed. Captivated by what they saw, Balinese youth were quick to take up surfing.

While many Balinese would benefit economically from surfing-inspired tourism, they would also pay dearly for its effect on their culture and environment. Pollution caused by the burning of plastics, the high volume of sewage from hotels and the draining of the water table were now posing serious threats to the future of the island. A small but telling example of this environmental degradation could be found in the cave which provided the only access to the surf at Uluwatu: for decades, surfers had been fouling their own nest by shitting there. The Surfrider Foundation – surfing's international environmental organisation – was trying to put an end to this practice by having toilets built nearby.

As someone who was conscious of the 'evil spirits' that came with development, Rusty was defensive about the changes that surfing had brought to Bali. 'Uluwatu used to be a dry, desolate, abandoned peninsula,' he said. 'Now they have surf hotels, water systems and so on. A lot of good relationships were established between surfers and the Balinese. Surfers became friends with people living in poor areas and went back year after year. Through those relationships and the development of surfing culture, the Balinese were able to build up ecotourism. Bali became our Hawaii.'

But if Bali had become 'our' Hawaii, what did that say about us? Like the USA in Hawaii, we had assumed the neo-colonial role, although our power is exercised through tourism, rather than annexation; an invasion of a different kind. An Australian surfer I met later would put it more bluntly. 'Australian surfers have taken their culture to Bali and ruined an indigenous culture almost single-handed.'

Melinda and I were dressing to go out to dinner when we saw the evening news. Another refugee boat bound for Christmas Island had sunk, this time with the loss of three hundred and fifty-three out of three hundred and ninety-seven passengers. The prime minister announced that the boat sank in Indonesian waters and was not Australia's responsibility. (It would emerge, in time, that the tragedy happened in international waters, well within Australia's surveillance zone.)

I sat down, half-dressed, on my bed, and wondered how differently the story might have been covered if the people in the boat had been Australians. A later item reported a drop in the number of toddlers drowning in pools. As the mother of a toddler, it was news that I was pleased to hear. But something unnerved me about the conjunction of the two items: what a gulf between the efforts we made to protect our own children from drowning, and the tardiness of our efforts to save refugee children drowning in our collective 'backyard'.

The day before we were to leave, Melinda and I went for a walk through the small rainforest that covers Cape Byron. It had been unseasonably dry for months and the usually lush undergrowth of forest palms and tree ferns was sparse and desiccated. The track wound its way up to the lighthouse on a rocky promontory at the easternmost tip of the continent. Passing this headland on 15 May 1770, Captain Cook wrote in his journal: 'a tolerable high point of land bore north west, distant three miles; this point I named Cape Byron'. The driving north-easterly wind and spitting rain made it too unpleasant to linger on the cape, but as we stood there, looking out to sea, with the swell bearing down from the Pacific, I was conscious of how this journey back to the water was inexorably drawing me out into that vastness.

I had met a local surfer, Captain Ronald Ware, whose connections with the Pacific, as a descendant of William Bligh, harked back to the beginnings of the colonial era. Red-cheeked and barrel-chested, Ron was no flowerchild. At seventy-six, he had the bluff, worldly air of an old sea dog, and called himself a 'professional survivor'. But he was more haunted by the past than he first appeared. He detailed his survival experiences without apparent distress: how he lost five ships when serving with the British Merchant Navy during World War Two; how he spent five days on a raft in the Indian Ocean with four other men before they were picked up and taken to Durban. 'When others lost their lives, I was fit and survived. I was the youngest but I took charge because I had that nature.' In Durban, surfing helped him recover. 'All these British troops used to stand on the jetty and watch me body surf. I've been a survivor ever since.'

It was no wonder that Ron identified with his famous forebear. After years spent working all over the world as a ship's captain, he finally realised his dream of re-enacting Captain William Bligh's open-boat voyage from Tonga to Timor after the mutiny on the *Bounty*. On 28 April 1789, Bligh along with eighteen of his men were forced off the ship by mutineers and set adrift with enough provisions for five days. It would be forty-two days before they would reach the Dutch settlement at Timor.

Ron's re-enactment voyage offered a way of imagining a moment early in the colonisation of the Pacific when a European, used to the trappings of authority and power that shielded him from the full brunt of the sea, was forced into a much more intimate relationship with the Pacific; one that was closer to the Polynesian experience than that of a nation which sought to rule, rather than ride, the waves. Unlike European sailors, for whom the ocean was an adversary (many could not swim), Polynesians were as at ease and intimate with the sea as they were on land. This was reflected in the design of their respective sea craft. The ethnohistorian Tommy Holmes argues that while Europeans 'almost blindly transposed concepts of land-based architecture to a very dissimilar marine environment', the boat design of the Pacific peoples was much more attuned to their watery world. Polynesian double-hulled voyaging canoes appeared shockingly fragile to European eyes, yet they often proved more flexible, manoeuvrable and faster than the more cumbersome European vessels. Such canoes, especially in Hawaii, were specifically designed to allow access to deep-sea fishing areas and to navigate the swell that regularly pounded the islands. The survival of Polynesian culture was, then, directly linked to the surfing ability of its ocean-going craft.

Ron's most vivid surfing experience during the reenactment occurred in the Coral Sea. Cyclonic winds whipped up an already heavy swell, and Ron and his crew soon found themselves in violently breaking seas riding waves of up to ten metres with craggy, overhanging crests. As he would write:

> . . . there was no alternative other than to run before
> the sea, quartering across the waves when possible

but putting our stern squarely to the sea when unable
to escape the breaking walls. The first time we surfed
a wave, I did not expect to survive it. The sea arched
high above us, lifting the stern to the sky, then broke,
with a roar, over our heads into the cockpit. At the
same moment we shot down the wave at high speed
with the surf running beside us and over the spray
dodger. My years of riding surf boats and surfboards
were now focused in reflex responses. The following
two waves in that set of three were ridden in the same
manner. Thrilling in concept but horrifying in reality.

Before the mutiny, while the *Bounty* was anchored for five
months at Matavai Bay in Tahiti, Bligh observed Tahitians
surfing out on the reef:

> The heavy surf which has run on the shore for a few
> days past has given great amusement to many of the
> Natives, but is such as one would suppose would
> drown any European. The general plan of this
> diversion is for a number of them to advance with their
> Paddles to where the Sea begins to break and, placing
> the broad part under the Belly, holding the other end
> with their Arms extended full length, they turn
> themselves to the surf and balancing themselves on
> the Paddles are carried to the shore with the greatest
> rapidity. The delight they take in this amusement
> is beyond anything and is of the most essential good

for them, for even in their largest and best Canoes they are so subject to accidents of being overturned that their lives depend on their swimming and habituating themselves to remain long in the water.

Here, Bligh is not just describing what he saw but acknowledging that Tahitians and Europeans had very different relationships with the sea. What gave the former 'great amusement' would surely drown 'any European'. Whereas the Tahitians were in their element in the heavy surf, Bligh was conscious above all of its dangers. To belong to a proud seafaring empire was one thing, but to be at home in the water, as the Polynesians were, was quite another. And yet survive Bligh did.

But survival, as Ron well knew, came at a cost. Towards the end of our long conversation, I asked him more about the war. With barely concealed agitation, he replied, 'I lost a lot of friends, good friends. I don't want to talk about it any more.' At that moment I could see the young sailor adrift at sea amid the debris of his ship, determined to block out the horror around him and bent on staying alive.

On the bus from Byron Bay to the airport at Coolangatta, I listened to the young backpackers who filled the seats around us with the hum of adventure, and found myself thinking of the surfing pilgrimages I had taken in my late teens and early twenties. All these trips were made with my boyfriend at the time, who was also a surfer. I remembered a rainy January spent travelling around Tasmania searching fruitlessly for surf. I remembered Cactus, a near-mythical desert surf beach in South Australia, near the West Australian border, where I sat in the dunes reading George Eliot's *Adam Bede*. What remained with me of Cactus was not the surf but the feeling of profound dislocation I experienced as I struggled to enter Eliot's rustic, nineteenth-century world of high-minded Methodists and fallen women, while sitting in a deckchair overlooking a stretch of ocean haunted by great white sharks. I remembered crossing the Nullarbor and camping at Esperance, the first town after hundreds of kilometres of desert, and how the passing semi-trailers carrying wheat to the harbour at night became massive, rumbling waves rolling through my dreams. I remembered days when the temperature soared to 42 degrees and we surfed until the glare from the aquamarine water almost blinded us.

During all those journeys, I was conscious of the split be-tween the part of me that loved this kind of surfing adventure and the part that was left desolate by these wild, remote coastlines, these frontier places. It wasn't that I hankered for the material comforts of civilisation (as I knew it) so much as for the psychological comfort of its culture and history, and the sense of belonging they gave.

Byron Bay might not be a great cultural or historical centre, but it did thrive on a spirit of enlightenment, tolerance and good will. Its solace was that it had managed, better than any-where else I knew, to marry paradise and civilisation. Perhaps 'marry' was too strong a word. A truce had been reached.

CHAPTER 6

Paradise Paved

AUTUMN / SPRING

Why shouldn't there be 'surfs' up on land?

'Surf Chant for Queen Emma'

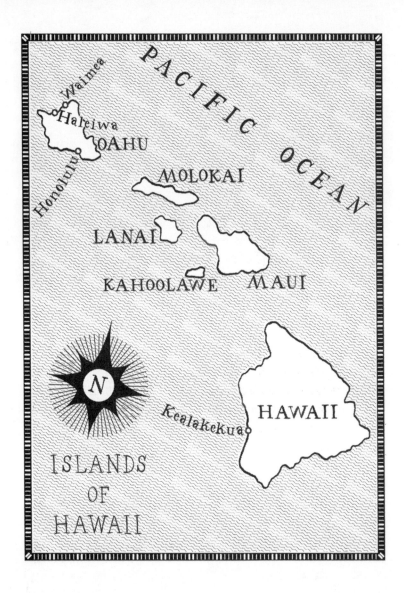

THE THREE OF us were sitting in a small Vietnamese restaurant on one of Honolulu's busiest avenues: Jack, his son Carl and I. The image of Carl as a five-year-old playing on the sand at Bells while Jack struggled for his life in the shorebreak had been so fixed in my mind that, until meeting Carl two days ago at the airport, I'd found it hard to imagine him as an adult. He was now a deep-voiced, twenty-seven-year-old engineer, almost a head taller than his father. Not surprisingly, he had grown up sharing Jack's love of the surf and the open ocean. For both father and son, Hawaii was a kind of ancestral home; their connection with the local culture – both surfing and seafaring – ran much deeper than mine. I was here because of the magnetic pull of the Pacific, and because Hawaii was where a surfing odyssey inexorably leads.

It was mid-March, early autumn at home, but here in the northern hemisphere winter was shading into spring. During the winter months storms sweep across the North Pacific and generate Hawaii's biggest swells, especially on the north shore of the island of Oahu at Waimea Bay and Sunset Beach. March was, then, a reasonably good time to be in Hawaii if you wanted to witness the kind of action that made these islands the region of Oceania where surfing evolved into an art form. Seeing big waves wasn't essential to the success of our trip, but being keenly swell-deprived, we couldn't help hoping.

The past year in Victoria had seen the worst surfing conditions that Jack could remember. No one seemed to know what meteorological forces had robbed us of summer, but by early autumn the vineyards of the Mornington Peninsula were heavy with unripened fruit and, on the opposite coast, Russell McConachy was still waiting, with mounting agitation, for a solid swell to bring Two Mile to life. He had never experienced a big wave famine like it. Time and again I would ring Jack for word on the surf at Torquay only to be told that it wasn't worth the journey. Either there was no swell or a south-easterly wind was messing up what little swell there was. 'Ever since you started this book,' Jack remarked, 'the surf hasn't been the same.'

Eighteen months before, I had returned to surfing confident that I was embarking on an adventure that would throw up challenges and ordeals similar to a sea voyage, moments of triumph and wonder, as well as a sense of striking out into a new way of life. I had imagined I would emerge mentally and physically stronger and, above all, more content with myself and the world. I had expected that I would achieve some kind of balance between my city life and coastal life, that my forays to the surf would fall into a natural rhythm a bit like the tides. During the first six months, those expectations had appeared realistic. With time, as I readjusted my outlook and focused less on my destination – surfing Corsair – and more on the journey and each moment within it, I felt I was beginning to fathom the deeper lessons that surfing had to offer. But as liberating as it is to be freed from the tyranny of progress, only a Buddhist monk can totally jettison the need for a sense of momentum and direction, the possibility of change: everything that the metaphor of the journey suggests.

What I hadn't counted on was finding myself trapped in the doldrums, my confidence slowly ebbing away as I waited for the conditions to improve. In my *Brewer's Dictionary of Phrase and Fable*, 'the doldrums' was described as 'a condition of depression, slackness or inactivity; hence applied by sailors to regions where ships were likely to be becalmed, especially those parts of the ocean near the Equator'. This entry sat between *dolce far niente* – 'delightful idleness' – and *dole* – 'lamentation' – from the latin *dolor*, meaning grief, sorrow. Like the doldrums, I was marooned between those two states, knowing neither the sweetness of the former nor the keen intensity of the latter.

My son – now a boisterous three-year-old – had taken to stacking pillows on the floor and putting a large, plastic tray on top of them. He would lie on the tray and jump to his feet saying, 'Look, Mama, I'm on a wave!' before going into a wobble and flamboyantly diving off. Watching him reminded me of an elderly surfer I had met who, when he couldn't get to the surf, would place his board on wedges of foam on the lounge room floor and practise leaping to his feet while watching TV. This, I feared, was what my surfing adventure might come to. But if I thought that I was stuck in the doldrums, the daily newspapers with their regular reports of refugee misery in detention centres – hunger strikes, rioting, self-mutilation, suicide attempts – put my dissatisfaction into perspective. What had happened to the life-changing journey that the boat people had so riskily embarked upon months or years before? If anyone was stuck on the *dolor* side of the doldrums, they were.

It was during this imposed lull, this period of treading water and waiting for the Southern Ocean to awaken from its torpor, that I again felt the pull of the Pacific, this time much stronger than before. These days, if one was fortunate enough to be born in the right country, and to have the money and the freedom to travel, one did not have to languish in the doldrums. Ever since I had first seen Webber's painting of Kealakekua Bay in the Surfworld Museum, and pondered what surfing had come to represent to the modern world, I had half known that I would have to go to Hawaii, back to where it all began.

Carl and Jack were on a high. They had spent the afternoon working on the Hokulea, Hawaii's first modern replica of an ancient sailing canoe. In 1976, the Hokulea sailed to Tahiti navigated by traditional techniques – the stars, the ocean currents and the flight of birds. The voyage had helped spark a renaissance in traditional Hawaiian culture, and now the knowledge of celestial navigation and the ancient art of canoe-building was being passed on to a new generation of Hawaiians.

The Polynesians' seafaring knowledge and canoe technology had allowed them to turn the borderless, blue unknown of the Pacific into a web of familiar seaways, long before the Vikings made their first raids. And according to Tommy Holmes, canoes were integral to the history of surfing: the Hawaiians were the only Pacific people to surf their craft purely for recreational pleasure. They also dreamed up the taxing art of *lele wa'a* or canoe leaping, a kind of ancient version of tow-in surfing in which a surfer would leap, with his board, from a canoe onto a wave as it began to crest, and then ride the board to shore.

As we waited for our main course to arrive, Jack, who still sailed regularly, said he'd not expected to be so moved by the documentary we'd seen at the Maritime Museum about the voyages of the *Hokulea*. We'd learned, among other things, of present-day Hawaiian navigators who blend modern science and tradition. In a stirring finale, the narrator told how the voyages of the *Hokulea* throughout Polynesia had linked the many scattered islands into one great *lei*, the traditional Hawaiian garland of flowers.

Jack was leaning forward, gesturing with his hands as he so often did to make a point. Normally the words came easily but tonight he was grappling for them, as he tried to explain why this ancient system of navigation meant so much to him. As a sailor, he was naturally enthralled by the history of Polynesian seafaring; but there was more to it than that. He liked the self-sufficiency of the old way. It threw sailors back on their own resources – on their intimate, visceral knowledge of the ocean in all its moods, along with the heavens and the winds. All these elements made Polynesian navigation a powerful symbol of life's journey.

'It's about finding your way back home,' Jack said looking keenly at Carl and me as if he feared that we would miss his point. 'Back to somewhere you feel you belong.'

Jack had talked to me of the devastating impact of being sent to boarding school as a young child, and how it left him with what he called 'a black hole in the head'. This black hole was a legacy that both he and his wife, Sue, shared. Sue had been four when she was sent off to boarding school; Jack seven. At the time, neither had been able to comprehend why they had been banished from everything and everyone they had ever loved. It was hardly surprising, then, that the symbolism of traditional navigation – a skill that gave you the inner resources to find your way home – should resonate so deeply with Jack.

The thrill of laying eyes on Diamond Head – the famous tapering from an extinct volcano that frames Waikiki Beach – remained with Jack. For him, Diamond Head represented the myth of the South Seas, that alluring, never-never land created by Melville, London, Stevenson, Conrad and all the other writers who had shaped his youthful dreams of paradise. Jack knew that his images of the Pacific were the products of escapist romanticism and that they had become tourist clichés. He was aware of the economic and political realities here, and he didn't like the way the Hawaiians had been treated, or that tourism and the US military called all the shots on the islands. And, sure, he found Waikiki pretty tacky. But none of these things could take away the pleasure that seeing it gave him.

Diamond Head had no associations whatsoever for me. My first reaction to it was disbelief that any government would allow an ugly big tourist development to be built on the very tip of such a significant natural feature. As we wandered up the beach on our first morning, a Celtic band with bagpipes was playing to stunned-looking guests breakfasting in a courtyard at one of the many beachfront hotels. Hotel staff wove between the tables, sweeping sand that had crept up from the beach back to where it belonged; it must have required eternal vigilance to keep the unruly trappings of the ocean at bay. The palms that lined the beach, swaying gently seaward with the off-shore wind, and the sapphire water – where one-foot waves rippled over the gradually sloping coral reef that produced Waikiki's famous rollers – were all that remained of the beach as it had been at the turn of the twentieth century, when surfing was revived here at the eleventh hour.

When describing the development of surfing, historians invariably invoke images of human evolution. Surfing in most of the islands throughout Polynesia, Macronesia and Micronesia was largely confined to body boarding – riding a wave prone on a short wooden board – although there are records of surfers kneeling on their boards in Tahiti and sometimes standing for a moment. But in Hawaii, as Ben Finney and James Houston describe it in their book, *Surfing: The Sport of Hawaiian Kings*, 'Pacific surfing reached its peak. There the feat of standing erect on a speeding surfboard found its noblest expression.' Not only did the Hawaiians elevate the act of surfing to an art form, they also wove it into their social customs, sexual practices and religious rituals, and celebrated it in their mesmerising oral literature and chants.

Other writers have taken this idea of the ascent of 'surfing man' even further. For Jack London, who visited Hawaii during his cruise on the *Snark* in 1907, a surfer was more than a man at the pinnacle of evolution. He was a god. 'Erect, full-statured, not struggling frantically in that wild movement, not buried and crushed and buffeted by those mighty monsters, but standing above them all, calm and superb, poised on the giddy summit, his feet buried in the churning foam, the salt smoke rising to his knee, and all the rest of him in the free air and flashing sunlight, and he is flying through the air, flying forward, flying fast as the surge on which he stands. He is a Mercury — a brown Mercury. His heels are winged, and in them is the swiftness of the sea . . . ' If Oceania was the cradle of surfing, Hawaii was its Athens.

After Cook's arrival at Kealakekua Bay, where Webber drew the first European image of a figure on a surfboard, it did not take long for surfing, like many other aspects of Hawaiian culture, to go into a steep and almost irretrievable decline. The upheavals that followed European intervention in the political and social structure of the islands saw the collapse, in 1819, of the *kapu* (taboo) system that underpinned Hawaiian religion and governed every aspect of society. When the gods fled, traditional practices lost their coherence and meaning. The annual Makahiki festival, which was being celebrated when Cook arrived, and public tournaments which had fostered activities like surfing were no longer held. What Finney and Houston call the 'sacred elements in the sport' – surf chants, board construction rites, sports gods – all disappeared with the erosion of indigenous religion. Western missionaries rushed to fill the void and did not look kindly upon the sexual freedom, gambling, and nakedness associated with surfing. Introduced diseases that decimated the native population and the Westerners' puritan emphasis on self-improvement rather than recreation also hastened surfing's decline.

By 1900, surfers were almost an extinct breed. A handful still paddled out at Waikiki, but having been stripped of its cultural significance, the sport had regressed. By the beginning of the twentieth century, the boards were basic, and the surfers lacked the technique and panache that had distinguished their forebears in the water. What saved the sport were the efforts of a few dedicated individuals, primarily the Irish-Hawaiian George Freeth, who later took surfing to America, the American Alexander Hume Ford, who conducted surfing classes at Waikiki, and the native Hawaiian surfer Duke Kahanamoku, who became the symbolic father of international surfing.

As we walked along Waikiki Beach one hundred years later, the latter-day beneficiaries of that revival, known as beach boys, were setting up their racks of surfboards for hire outside their booths under the palms. Down past the pink confection of the Royal Hawaiian Hotel and the Edwardian stateliness of the Moana, we stopped at a booth and hired ourselves waterlogged, ten-foot planks which were so heavy that we had to drag them to the water's edge. Waikiki's gently spilling waves are ideal for beginners and many surfers were out; there was no escaping the fact that surfing was part of the tourist package here. Because the waves were so easy to catch, surfing was just one of the many recreational activities, like snorkelling or golf, that the tourist could sample. We joined the hordes in the water and lazed about in the sun on our massive, weighty planks, occasionally catching a wave and joking that we could hold a conference as we cruised languidly shorewards side by side. The surf was hardly challenging but to be riding the famous waves we had seen in surfing footage was thrilling in itself.

A seventeen-foot bronze statue of Duke Kahanamoku stands on the beachfront, his arms outstretched in an eternal gesture of aloha as the surf of Waikiki rolls behind him. It was Kahanamoku, an Olympic swimmer and dedicated surfer, who introduced surfing to Australia in 1914, when he came to Freshwater Beach in Sydney to give a swimming exhibition. After fashioning himself an eight-foot board from solid American sugar pine bought from a local timberyard, Kahanamoku put on a surfing demonstration. He asked for someone to ride tandem with him, and the surf lifesaving club 'volunteered' a fifteen-year-old called Isabel Letham who was known as a fine bodysurfer and ocean swimmer. The experience turned her into a lifelong surfer, and the demonstration was hailed as the greatest spectacle of its kind ever witnessed in Australia.

Whenever I thought about Isabel Letham, I couldn't help wistfully imagining an alternative history of Australian surfing in which women, right from the beginning, played an equal part, as women had done in ancient Hawaii. A history in which girls like Isabel took to the waves with as much confidence, encouragement and abandon as the eager boys who went on to make Australia one of the leading surfing nations.

Still not quite awake from an afternoon nap, my brain fogged by the early stages of yet another cold, I force-marched my way down Waikiki's glitzy beachfront shopping strip, which is overshadowed by high-rise apartments and hotels. The cold had affected my sense of balance and the ground felt spongy beneath my feet, as if I had just stepped ashore after a long session in the surf. When I looked skywards, the buildings swayed. I dodged my way through the crowds of shoppers, my head jangling with the lyrics of Joni Mitchell's 'Big Yellow Taxi': 'They paved paradise and put up a parking lot.'

I had a rendezvous at Duke Kahanamoku's statue with one of his protégés, Rabbit Kekai, who caught his first wave here in 1925 at the age of five. In photographs from around 1910, Waikiki Beach has the atmosphere of a rural village, with grass huts on the sand flanked by massive banyan trees. When the Moana Hotel first went up in 1901, the beach was still a swampy marshland of taro patches and rice paddies. Not long after, the area was reclaimed. By the time Rabbit started surfing, tourism had accelerated, especially after the opening of Waikiki's other famous luxury hotel, the Royal Hawaiian, in 1927. But all this was still a far cry from the present-day jungle of concrete and glass.

Rabbit and I found a spot on the foreshore lawn – I in the sun because I was cold, Rabbit in the shade because he knew it was stupid to sit in the Hawaiian sun if you didn't have to. Although his hooded eyelids gave him a sleepy air, his dark eyes were watchful. We talked briefly about how things had changed at Waikiki, but Rabbit wasn't much inclined to indulge in nostalgia or to mourn the disappearance of old Waikiki. 'You can't buck progress. It doesn't bother me. Living in this age, you have to adapt.'

And adapt he had. He was best known as an early surfing innovator and was now regarded as the father of modern 'hot dogging' – manoeuvring on the nose of the board. For all that, he had little desire to live off his past glories. He proudly mentioned a television advertisement he had recently appeared in and how well he had been paid. He wanted it known that at eighty-one he was still a tough competitor, and still in demand. Having spent his days inhabiting the eternal now of Waikiki Beach, it was important to him that he remained a man of the moment.

The beach boys at Waikiki were among the first to take advantage of surfing's commercial possibilities. Rabbit had capitalised on his superb physique, surfing ability and considerable knowledge of the ocean. Long before surfing became a professional sport, he had made surfing and the beach his profession. To be a beach boy was to be a showman. It meant performing with beautiful young gymnasts perched on his shoulders and doing waterstunts in films like *The Old Man and the Sea*, *From Here to Eternity* and *Gidget Goes Hawaiian*. The work brought glamour and recognition. When the rich and famous – Gregory Peck, Kirk Douglas, the Shah of Iran, and others of their ilk – stayed at the Royal Hawaiian or the Moana and wanted a surfing instructor, they asked for Rabbit.

Rabbit was well aware of the value of his glamorous image but was keen to distinguish himself from the kind of beach boys who made their names as party boys. He was proud of having been singled out by Duke Kahanamoku, who took an interest in him after he won his first outrigger race as a junior steersman. But there was an Oedipal sting in his story of their relationship. Duke gave Rabbit advice, paid his entry fees to contests, and generally spurred him on – until Rabbit beat him in a canoe race by applying the tactics that Duke himself had taught him.

Rabbit reeled off the many paddleboard races, canoe and outrigger contests, and surfing competitions that he had won. I thought of Tennyson's 'Ulysses', where the ageing adventurer boasts of the famous exploits that have led him to 'become a name'. Like Ulysses, Rabbit was highly conscious of his reputation as a folk hero, of his status as 'a name' in Hawaiian surfing. Until the late 1970s, the surfing world was not much interested in reflecting on its past or honouring the achievements of its pioneers. It was dominated by wild young men who had little interest in what had come before them. Since then, the surfing population had aged, the longboard had been revived, and the surf industry had gone into overdrive to create a modern mythology replete with heroes and folklore.

As someone for whom surfing had always been a way of making a living as well as a way of life, Rabbit had no qualms about self-promotion. He knew what the tourists wanted and he was adept at giving it to them – a canny mixture of aloha and bravado. He brought out a folder and handed me a signed photograph of his younger self on a wave in a classic hotdog pose. The caption read, 'Rabbit Kekai, The Hawaiian Legend.'

For a time it seemed that our bus would never escape the endless industrial estates, military installations (Pearl Harbor in the distance) and uniform suburbs that consumed the hillsides on the outskirts of Honolulu. But slowly the houses gave way to pineapple and sugar plantations and ranches in a sea of green. After the grey sprawl of Honolulu, the north shore felt like another country: a taste of old Hawaii. Passing through Hale'iwa, a quiet hippy town of wild-west style buildings made of chocolate timber, we glimpsed the surf between the foreshore scrub. A pretty little turquoise bay overlooked by a Tuscan-style campanile with a terracotta roof came into view. Behind a wide beach of creamy sand lay a tea-coloured lagoon fed by a river that snaked through a lushly vegetated valley.

Jack reached over and tapped my knee. 'That's Waimea.'

From the late 1950s to the early 1990s – until the advent of tow-in surfing – Waimea was regarded as the Mount Everest of surf breaks. For those who knew anything about surfing, Waimea might as well have been Hawaiian for 'bloody monstrous'. I had read about the U-shaped bay, and how its dramatic volcanic surrounds dwarf the onlooker. I had read about the huge thick humps that rise like volcanoes from the sea, as the Hawaiian islands themselves had done, producing great bursts of foam and spray. I had read about the punishment these gigantic waves can inflict upon those reckless enough to tangle with them. Inevitably, the Waimea Bay in my head had acquired fearsome dimensions. I had pictured the coastal equivalent of Caspar David Friedrich's *The Wanderer above the Mists*, in which a frock-coated man standing on a rocky outcrop stares across a cloudy chasm towards distant mountain peaks. I imagined myself, like the Wanderer, looking down from steep, primeval cliffs of a grandeur commensurate with the monstrous cliffs of water toppling shorewards.

But now as I stared out the bus window, I found that the scale in my head was all wrong. Instead of descending to the beach from a great height, one reached it from road level. The bay itself was not awesome but intimate, no bigger than the cove at Sorrento back beach. Instead of surfers contending with giants of the sea, there were families swimming in the soft green water and kids jumping off the rocks. There was no surf at all.

I gaped at Jack. *This is Waimea?*

We sat on the foreshore, watching the water sucking at the dark, volcanic rocks, eating our lunch in silence. I thought about how we had come all this way in the faint hope of seeing a natural feature that was not really a feature at all. If you visited the Himalayas to see Mount Everest or went to Egypt to see the pyramids, you could be sure of success. But waves were mountains of the mind. There one day, gone the next.

'It must be a fearsome place when it's working,' said Carl, who had been absorbing the view of the water roiling about the rocks.

'There'd be spray flying up over those palms,' answered Jack, pointing to a spot forty metres back from the water. 'And the ground,' he patted the sand, 'would be shaking with the impact.'

Conjure up what it might be like: it was all we could do. I was starting to feel as if we were trapped in a scene from *Waiting for Godot*. Never had a trip to the surf felt more like a lesson in the Absurd – the perfect denouement to months of waiting for swell that never arrives. The odds of seeing really big waves were relatively small, but on any given day – especially at this time of year – one had reason to presume that Waimea might produce something at least resembling surf. To know that the water could be flat in the morning and thirty feet high in the afternoon was to live in hope. That eternal promise, that tantalising elusiveness was essential to surfing's appeal. It was what whetted your appetite for more, what kept boredom at bay. It was what made those perfect days so unforgettable. You had to be philosophical about it, had to find pleasure in the tease, or you would be forever on edge, permanently agitated by your lack of control. The key to serinty was making the most of what you were given.

Like Estragon and Vladimir, Jack and I sat on the sand talking about the meaning of waiting for surf. 'Even when nothing appears to be happening, something is,' Jack insisted. 'You're reading the ocean, making sense of it all. There's still plenty going on. If we'd come here with the single aim of catching waves we'd be pretty bloody miserable by now. But we didn't and we're not. We knew this was on the cards.'

I didn't want to admit it but as philosophical as I tried to be, I felt as if I'd come to a world-famous theatre to see a great epic only to find myself gazing at an empty stage. The analogy wasn't quite right – the sea was never empty, never still. It was always there to be enjoyed and contemplated. But today it was giving nothing away.

The Bishop Museum of Polynesian Culture possessed a large collection of old surfboards. Wandering through the warehouse where many of them were stored was like walking through the remnants of an ancient forest. Massive, antique koa boards, some over seventeen feet long, stood in racks; other lay prone, gathering dust. There were solid, polished wooden boards of various thicknesses and lengths that had once belonged to Hawaiian kings, queens and princesses; there were examples of early hollow, plywood boards; there were malibus made of balsa and fibreglass, and the first foam and fibreglass models.

As important as surfboard design is to the evolution of surfing – it determines the kind of waves one can catch and how they are ridden – the stories behind these boards were what most interested me. One of the boards – a shortish, flat-bottomed board – belonged to a mid-nineteenth-century princess who was said to sneak away from her family home at night to go surfing. The oldest known board, a small body board, belonged to a Big Island chiefess in the mid-1600s; made of the wood of the breadfruit tree, it was found in a burial cave. But the most memorable story was about a surfer of noble lineage who saw a beautiful 'dragon woman' out in the surf and eagerly climbed onto her board to make love to her. She lured him back to her cave and they made love for several months until his energy was sapped and, like Odysseus in the thrall of Calypso, he pined for home. When he told her he wanted to go surfing, she gave him her long, detachable tongue to use as a surfboard. The board, first an object upon which to surf and then a moving platform for lovemaking, had now become a symbol of unspeakable desire.

Wandering amongst these old tapered planks – which were flat at one end and rounded at the other – I was suddenly struck by their tongue-like appearance and by the aptness of the image. Surfing is undoubtedly a form of self-expression; but what does it express? The provenance of the 'oceanic feeling' suggests that the surfer's experience will always be difficult to articulate because it harks back to the earliest phase of infant development before language has been acquired; a phase in which the child experiences the breast, the mother and the world as an amorphous extension of the self. It could be argued, then, that the board tongue enacts some very basic, primal urges as it licks its way across the water, and is itself licked and fed by the wave. Only a language like Hawaiian, which is so finely tuned to the many nuances and moods of the sea, can come close to translating this experience into words. As well as meaning 'the surf' or 'a wave', the Hawaiian word *nalu* also means 'to speak secretly or to speak to oneself; to think within oneself.' You only had to watch the inward curl of a breaking wave, watch it folding into itself and hear its susurrations on the shore, to appreciate how a wave might suggest these metaphors. To engage with the breaking wave is, then, to participate in a secret form of communion, a silent regression into the hidden recesses of the self.

Yet in ancient Hawaii, that mute soliloquy was not only a form of individual self-expression, a source of personal pleasure or a solitary spiritual experience. It was part of a web of social and religious practices that involved the whole community. Offerings, blessings and incantations were all rituals associated with the making of boards and the selection of wood. There were temples dedicated to surfing and invocations to the gods that could be recited to bring up the surf. Entire villages could lie deserted when the surf was up as the men, women and children took to the water. Formal courtships were carried out in the surf, and if a man and a woman caught the same wave, custom allowed 'certain intimacies' when they returned to the beach. Spectators at surfing contests often gambled heavily, wagering their canoes, swine, fishing nets and sometimes their lives or freedom. Hawaiian lore records how these competitions sometimes ended in the death of participants, especially when the contest was between rival chiefs.

The surfing feats of the chiefly class, who took their surfing very seriously, were celebrated in surfing chants or *mele*. These *mele* were delivered by a *kahu* or chanter who was part of the chief's or chiefess' retinue. One of the most renowned surfing legends tells of the surf chant of a champion surfer and orator who became the governor of the island of Hawaii. Known as Naihe Haiha, he rose to prominence in the early decades of the nineteenth century. Naihe's fellow chiefs, it was said, were jealous of his surfing ability and plotted to do away with him during a surfing contest. They agreed that none of the chiefs could return to the beach until each one's personal chant was recited from the shore; any chief who broke the rule would be killed. Once Naihe was out in the surf, he realised that he had fallen into their trap, so he remained in the water all day until night began to fall. Finally, Naihe's *kahu*, an old woman, rushed to the beach and, with tears streaming down her face, began to chant. Her chant was judged the best and Naihe was allowed to live.

This story, where a surfer's life hangs on the recital of a poem, has no modern equivalent. Sitting in the museum archives surrounded by documents and books in which surfing and poetry were interfused, I felt at home for the first time since arriving in Hawaii. As a teenager, my dream of the ideal existence had been to live by the sea, go surfing and write poetry. I had always thought of the two activities as intimately related, even though there was little in modern surf culture to encourage such an idea. Now, at last, here was a surf culture that made sense to me. And so it happened that my Hawaiian surfing epiphany took place in a room full of books and not the green room of the sea.

The librarian helping me with my search placed one of Naihe's chants before me. It had been adopted after Naihe's death by King Kalakaua, who took the throne in 1874 and who promoted the revival of many ancient Hawaiian cultural practices, including the *hula* and chants. In this particular version, the hero of the chant is King Kalakaua rather than Naihe. It opens with Kane, the god of light, life and water, surfing from island to island until he arrives at the island of Papa, the female progenitor of humans. The chant ends stirringly with King Kalakaua riding to shore bruised (but not bloodied) on his broken board:

> The first full grown wave arises,
> The second full grown wave is the crafty one,
> The third full grown wave spreads over,
> The fourth full grown wave rushes onward;
> The dusty one mounts and rides the board,
> The sea is streaked red by the board of the chief.
> It arrives at his home among the budding flowers.

Light-headed, I picked up the other chant the librarian had found me, one dedicated to King Kalakaua's political rival, Queen Emma, widow of Kamehameha IV. After her son's death, Emma and Kalakaua campaigned against one another for succession to the throne and Emma lost. While no date was given for 'Surf Chant for Queen Emma', one line in particular – 'It is because of ignorance that the chiefs deny that this is a chiefess' – suggests that the chant was composed after Emma's defeat. In the chant, Queen Emma's domain over the land, the sea and the heavens is constantly reiterated through the image of her surfing between these realms.

As I read the chant and fell under its spell, I knew I had found my surfing patron saint. Modern surfing has been largely a male preserve and, at its worst, hostile to women surfers. Yet in early Hawaii, women were a common sight in the surf and were just as skilled as the men. Engravings and drawings of surfing by early visitors to Hawaii show women and men surfing in equal numbers. In many ways, Queen Emma was one of the last in this ancient line of women who took surfing for granted.

While Emma was steeped in Victorian ideas of refinement (she had a Western education and became a friend of Queen Victoria's after visiting Britain), she was also deeply rooted in Hawaiian culture. In traditional Hawaii style, her chant celebrates her as a sexual being:

> Red hot is the 'surf' of the chiefess,
> Rising in billows are the 'surfs' of the chiefess,

Quaking, reverberating, the gods rumble
And stand on the inclining 'surf' of Mauna Kea,
Mauna Loa and Hualalai.

For Queen Emma, surfing is not just a healthy and invigorating pastime, as it might have been construed in Victorian times. Surfing is a metaphor for understanding and experiencing the world and symbolic of a life force that connects all things:

The *holua* sledding is a 'surf' of Waiakanonoulai,
The horse and buggy is a 'surf' up on the land,
The earthquake is a 'surf' that shakes the earth,
The rainbow is a 'surf' and so is the low lying
      rainbow on the ocean,
The awa[1] planted by the birds on a tree is a 'surf',
The popolo and the laulele weeds are 'surfs',
Upon which men and women glide,
The old women and the old men surf,
And land, land on the surf of Mauliola.[2]

---

[1] native kava shrub
[2] a god of health

Other metaphorical 'surfs' or 'surf breaks' include the raised place in a temple called the *kapaau* where offerings are placed. The rising sun is also said to be a surf in the ocean, 'rising high toward the sky'.

I knew that there were all sorts of political and cultural references in the chant that I would probably never fathom. 'A 'surf' is the water in the mirage of Mana, on land,' the chant declares. *Mana* means 'desert' but it also means 'to have power'. Was this a reference to power being a mirage? Or that Queen Emma could ride the elusive waves of power with the same mastery that she could surf? Surfing was, after all, one of the ways in which the ancient chiefs asserted their authority. The final part of the chant invites the latter reading, as it extends the surfing metaphor to places that Queen Emma visited after her husband's death:

A place to surf is at France,
The last of the 'surfs' is America,
The force that carries the 'surfs' along is Russia,
The place where the surf lands is England.
They are the distant 'surfs' of the islands. Come home,
We think they are the surfs of the chiefess,
The sun rises, coming up at Ha'eha'e,
Over the Pacific, Atlantic, Indian and Arctic oceans.

By 'surfing' the places mentioned here, Queen Emma demonstrates her skills in international diplomacy, her royal influence, her symbolic dominion. 'The surf' is a highly malleable conceit that connects inner drives – sexual urges, hunger, the desire for power – with cosmic forces. To surf is to live exultantly, to venture confidently into the wider world, to celebrate the interconnectedness of all things.

The idea of Queen Victoria surfing is an amusing one. Yet for Hawaiians there was nothing strange or laughable about a royal figure like Queen Emma surfing. To realise this is to appreciate what surfing meant in Hawaii: that it could be political, physical, spiritual; that it was once integral to Hawaiian experience in a way it can no longer be in the modern world.

My head reeling, I gathered up my copies of the chants. As limited as my understanding of them was, they had already given me much more than I'd dared hope for. In their complex and expansive use of surfing as a metaphor, in their epic understanding of the surf as an arena for the full range of life's experiences from comedy to tragedy, in the way they tapped into the very rhythms of the ocean, they had transformed my understanding of what the 'idea of surfing' might mean. And, as if answering my anxieties about having missed out on the surf while in Hawaii, these chants swept me up on a wave of their own making. It was indeed possible to surf upon the land.

I first saw John Kelly in a documentary by David L. Brown called *Surfing for Life* about a group of Hawaiian and American surfers aged between sixty and ninety. There was something about John, an air of quiet dignity, thoughtfulness and contained passion that made me want to meet him.

A big wave pioneer and long-time activist, John was now in his early eighties. In the 1960s, as new freeways began ripping up old communities, and as tourist development encroached upon surfing breaks and fishing areas, John and some friends founded the environmental organisation Save Our Surf (SOS).

He lived in the house his parents had built, now part of an affluent, gated community at Black Point in Honolulu. His welcome was warm if somewhat distracted. In the dark, wooden-panelled lounge, his crisp blue Hawaiian shirt and luminous sea-blue eyes were the brightest things in the room. Jack and I would have to speak up, he explained, as his hearing was not good. At one end of the room there was a cloth-covered grand piano weighed down with books and ornaments. John had been a music teacher and conductor but the piano looked like it had not been played for years. The walls were hung with etchings and watercolours by his father, while the sideboards and tables held his mother's bronze sculptures and busts.

Books lined the walls of his small study, and on the floor sat stacks of journals and yellowed SOS pamphlets from four decades of campaigns against tourist and urban developments that threatened the Hawaiian coastline. Propped on a shelf was a photograph of Chairman Mao. It was clear from John's writings that his analysis of society was deeply influenced by Marx. Yet the form Marxism took in SOS was vastly different from its autocratic application by Mao or Lenin. SOS was a fluid, non-centralised organisation befitting the anarchic temperaments of most surfers. It had many thousands of participants but no membership or constitution; no elected leaders or internal structure. This was heady, idealistic stuff that could easily be dismissed as naive in the hard-nosed twenty-first century, but it had worked. SOS had put a stop to an impressive range of potentially damaging coastal developments all over Hawaii, including breakwaters, tourist resorts, golf courses, freeways and power plants.

Dilco, one of the major construction companies in Hawaii, had once planned to build a tunnel under Black Point and then a ten-mile freeway across the reefs from Black Point to Koko Head. John looked at us with shining eyes. 'We put out thousands of leaflets. The people living along the beaches here were mostly local people. Boy, were they mad and we stopped it.'

He led us around his desk to the window that looked out over Maunalua Bay to Koko Head. Jack and I gaped at the view. How could anyone dream up such an outlandish, ugly and environmentally devastating plan for such a beautiful bay? And yet, you only had to look at Waikiki to realise that nothing was inconceivable to those in the construction industry.

As I passed John's desk, I noticed some newspaper clippings on it. They were articles about Alzheimer's disease. A number of times he had struggled to find the right words. Once, he cried out in frustration, 'What's wrong with my brain?' A rhetorical question, as he clearly knew the answer. Now he said simply, 'I have this problem with my memory.' The 'problem' was less apparent when he had some kind of *aide-mémoire*, a photograph or a pamphlet to jog his memory or to read from. But there were many aspects of his life that

John could no longer tell us about. He could speak generally about how waves were produced by storms in the Pacific and about the technicalities of board-making; he could tell us that the native Hawaiians had taught him how to hyperventilate to store up oxygen in his body when he had to dive under big waves. But he could not remember the names of his friends who had drowned when surfing.

He kept returning to two memories which seemed to hold special significance for him. The first was about skipping school when he was a boy and surfing all the way to Waikiki, then calling his mother to fetch him home. The second was about the experience of being inside a big wave. Demonstrating with his hands, he talked excitedly about travelling through the tube of a wave, how good it felt when it enclosed you and how sometimes you could ride inside it for a long distance. It seemed more than coincidental that both these 'spots of time' were surfing stories about returning home: whether to a literal home or to the wave as a kind of womb.

When I returned home a few days later, there was a bundle of books waiting for me to review. One of them was David Shenk's *The Forgetting*; it was subtitled *Understanding Alzheimer's: The Biography of a Disease*. I devoured the book and caught my breath when I came upon the poem 'Terminus' by the nineteenth-century American poet and transcendentalist Ralph Waldo Emerson. In his late sixties, Emerson went into a slow decline with what would now be recognised as Alzheimer's. The poem's resolute fearlessness in the face of encroaching oblivion – predicted by Emerson before anyone else was aware of it – was exactly what I had witnessed and been so moved by in John Kelly. Terminus, appropriately, is the Roman god of boundaries and landmarks:

> It is time to be old,
> To take in sail: –
> The god of bounds,
> Who sets to seas a shore,
> Came to me in his fatal rounds,
> And said, 'No more!'
> . . .
> As the bird trims her to the gale,
> I trimmed myself to the storm of time,
> I man the rudder, reef the sail,
> Obey the voice at eve obeyed at prime:
> 'Lowly faithful, banish fear,
> Right onward drive unharmed;
> The port, well worth the cruise, is near,
> And every wave is charmed.'

The road cut through vast lava beds wrinkled like elephant hide as Jack and I drove across the island of Hawaii, known as the Big Island, past the snow-capped peak of Mauna Kea, a now-extinct volcano. After the frenetic pace and urban sprawl of Honolulu, the Big Island was refreshingly empty and undeveloped. The lava beds made the deep past seem much closer, more immediate than elsewhere, as if the magma that had spurted to the surface centuries before had only just cooled. As we headed south toward Kealakekua Bay along the Kona coast, the arid, savanna-like landscape gave way to palms, hibiscus, banana plants and bougainvillea. The main road followed a high ridge on the lower reaches of Mauna Loa, and the descent to the coast was a dizzying, endless switchback of hairpin bends. Kealakekua Bay lay six kilometres south of the town of Captain Cook, but the side of the bay where Cook had been killed was inaccessible by car. The road took us down to the village of Napo'opo on the opposite headland and ended at the ruins of an ancient temple or *heiau*, the entrance to which was roped off with a sign announcing that this was a sacred site. It was the temple of Lono, the god of the Land, for whom Cook had been mistaken when he arrived at Kealakekua Bay.

Kealakekua was now a state marine life preserve prized for its brilliantly coloured fish, sea turtles and spinner dolphins. Jack and I stood staring across the water to the far side of the bay, where we could just make out the white plinth of the monument to Cook.

A large woman stepped forward from a group of Hawaiians who were sitting in deck chairs under a nearby tree. 'You want to go over there? I can rent you a kayak.'

We manoeuvred our boat off the coal-black lava rock and into the water. There was no sign of swell, and so deep and protected was the bay that it was hard to imagine much swell ever making its way in. Yet the Kona coast, which had once been densely populated, was remembered as one of Hawaii's most heavily surfed areas. A map of surfing spots in ancient Hawaii, based on legends and early writings, indicates a number of surf breaks inside the bay not far from where Cook's ships were anchored. Lieutenant James King, who completed the final volume of Cook's *Voyage to the Pacific Ocean*, noted that the surf broke 'on the coast round the bay' and extended 'to the distance of about 100 and 50 yards from the shore'. This would seem to suggest that the surf broke inside the bay rather than just on the exposed coast on either side.

King proved to be a keen observer of the 'perilous' and 'extraordinary' art of surfing:

> Whenever, from stormy weather, or any extraordinary swell at sea, the impetuosity of the surf is increased to its utmost height, they choose that time for this amusement, which is performed in the following manner: 20 or 30 of the natives taking each a long, narrow board, rounded at the ends, set out together from the shore. The first wave they meet, they plunge under, and suffering it to roll over them, rise again beyond it, and make the best of their way by swimming out into the sea. The second wave is encountered in the same manner with the first; the great difficulty consisting in seizing the proper moment of diving under it, which, if missed, the person is caught by the surf and driven back again

with great violence; and all his dexterity is then
required to prevent himself from being dashed against
the rocks. As soon as they have gained, by repeated
efforts, the smooth water beyond the surf, they lie
themselves at length on their board and prepare for
their return. Their first object is to place themselves
on the summit of the largest surge, by which, they are
driven along with amazing rapidity toward the shore.
The coast being guarded by a chain of rocks, with,
here and there, a small opening between them, they
are obliged to steer their board through one of these
or, in case of failure, to quit it before they reach the
rocks, and plunging under the wave, make the best
of their way back again. This is reckoned very
disgraceful and is also attended with the loss of the
board, which I have often seen, with great terror,
dashed to pieces at the very moment the islander
quitted it. The boldness and address with which we
saw them perform these difficult and dangerous
manoeuvres was altogether astonishing and is
iscarcely to be credited.

From a distance the water had appeared dull beneath the
heavy grey sky, but as we glided over it in our kayak, we
found ourselves peering into lapis lazuli depths so darkly
luminous they seemed to be lit from below. Massive and sheer,
the volcanic, puce-coloured cliffs covered with pale green
tufts of vegetation reared up like a fortress to our right,

dividing the bay into two halves. Unlike Waikiki or even Waimea Bay, the primordial, brooding atmosphere of the place remained undisturbed by the few tourists who briefly flitted into the bay, scrambled over rocks, dipped their heads below the water and then departed. While there were houses set back in the hillside near the side of the bay from which we had come, there was none of the bustle and activity that King records.

Jack had brought with him a large copy of the engraving based on Webber's painting of Cook's arrival. He wanted to establish the perspective from which the artist had viewed the scene, in order to identify the position of the lone surfer in the foreground who is paddling out alongside a small fleet of outrigger canoes towards the British ships. This first Western image of a man on a board was a detail that was no doubt lost on most viewers. And yet it was this detail that had brought us here.

On the far side of the bay, we climbed out of the kayak and pulled it up onto the rocks. Almost nothing remained of the village of Kaawaloa. Jack held up the engraving and tried to align it with the surrounding coast. As a mariner, he liked to work out the lie of the land and the coast, and position himself in relation to it. This was his way of entering the historical moment depicted in Webber's painting. But whichever way we looked at it, the engraving wouldn't match up with our surroundings. We followed a short path through the trees to the Cook monument commemorating the 'great circumnavigator' (part of which had been defaced and then restored). Cook had been feted and worshipped as a god on the other side of the bay; he was killed here, when he returned ten days after leaving to fix a mast on *Resolution*. He had violated the role that the Hawaiians had assigned him in their cosmology – the god Lono was not supposed to return so soon.

We decided to go snorkelling. Barely a metre from the jagged, slippery volcanic rocks where Cook had fallen after being stabbed and beaten was a world unto itself. Here, beneath the surface, were the most unexpected visions of tropical paradise: fish flashing scales of neon pink and yellow; black fish with tangerine and blue trimming; ancient-looking turtles drifting up from the deep blue depths where the ocean floor fell precipitously away. In this small submarine enclave where a rainbow seemed to have bled into the water (as a Hawaiian chant might put it), one was deliciously free of the weight of human history that pressed down on one's shoulders on land; a history that scarred the landscape and the people in it. I briefly wondered if Cook had glimpsed this paradise when he lay face down in the water before darkness descended. Then I pushed the thought away.

I had come here to contemplate the confused and bloody colonial moment in which surfing entered Western conscious-ness only to find myself happy to forget about it. To just drift and feast my eyes and relish this buoyancy; this feeling of merging with the ocean, of having escaped the outside world, of being suspended in time. All the sensations that drew me to surfing. But I also knew from my surfing experience that this impulse to flee existed in exquisite tension with the need to confront disturbing events, whether the approach of a big wave or the pressure of history. Surfing might allow one to lose oneself in the eternal now, like that Tahitian canoeist Cook observed surfing at Matavai Bay; but the poignancy of Cook's sketch lay in our knowledge that the surfer's sanctuary was temporary, that while he could, for a short time, ignore the Europeans camped nearby, he would not escape their impact. Tellingly, these contradictions were contained within the complex nuances of *he'e nalu* – 'wave sliding', a term that seemed to keep unfolding like an intricate work of origami. *He'e* – to flee; *nalu* –'to think; to search after any truth or fact'.

It wasn't until Jack and I had paddled most of the way back that the realisation dawned: Webber's engraving showed the coast ahead, not the side of the bay where Cook had drowned. Now it all fell into place – the beach with the palm trees behind it, the rocky black outcrops that dominate the foreground, the way the cliffs taper away behind. The sandy part of the beach had disappeared but a small crescent of dark grey pebbles remained. The contrast in mood between Webber's picture and the eerie stillness of the place now was striking. It was the stillness of a graveyard. The only reminder of the throngs of Hawaiians in canoes and on surfboards who had rushed out to welcome Cook – not knowing that his appearance would usher in the end of their world – were three young boys on boogie boards catching small waves in the shorebreak.

CHAPTER 7

Civilised Surf?

WINTER / SUMMER

Now we draw near the centre of the civilized world . . . The huge uproar is in my ears. It sounds and resounds under this glass roof like the surge of a sea. We are cast down on the platform with our hand bags. We are whirled asunder. My sense of self almost perishes. I become drawn in, tossed down, thrown sky-high.

Virginia Woolf, THE WAVES

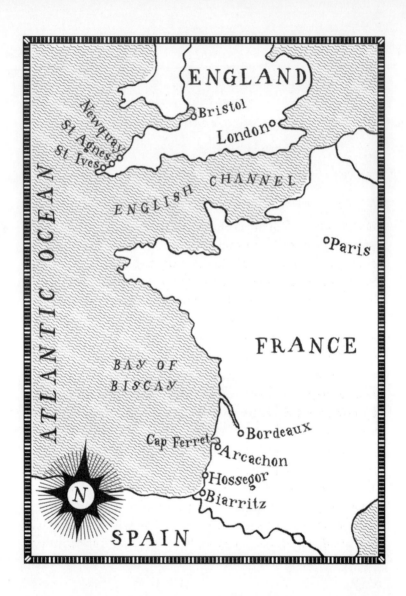

WHENEVER I TOLD non-surfers why I was going to Europe, they laughed. Most Australians had no idea that surf worthy of the name broke on the shores of the Old World. When last in Europe, I had been five months pregnant and supremely happy. Swimming around inside me, my son had kept me company as I hunted for fossils on the beaches of Gotland and watched a lone surfer trying to ride the wind-whipped meringue of the Baltic Sea; the boy's swelling presence a constant, joyful reminder of the great adventure ahead.

Four years later, as I contemplated the prospect of visiting Cornwall and the south-west of France, that spirit of adventure seemed to have abandoned me. In its place was a hard knot in my gut that would not go away. I would wake in the night asking myself what on earth I thought I was doing. It was not as if Europe was an obvious or essential destination for a surfing odyssey. Leaving my son to go to Hawaii was one thing, but travelling to the other side of the world was quite another.

I sat down on the couch with the boy and told him that I would be going away.

'It is far, far away where you're going?'

I had to admit that it was. 'But I'll be back very soon,' I said, knowing it would not be soon enough.

Reassured, his eyes flickered towards the television, where Maisy Mouse was in bed with her toy panda.

'Can you bring me back a panda?'

Once we had established that I would return bearing a panda, he showed no more desire to talk about the subject. His concept of time was still vague and I was not sure how much he understood about my approaching absence, but I felt that I'd got off rather lightly. When a friend told her five-year-old son that she would be away for two days, he said he felt 'as if there had been a death'. I understood what he meant. The prospect of separation from loved ones *can* feel horribly final, especially when air travel is involved. I began to have morbid, melodramatic thoughts that I would die or that something would happen to my son while I was away. Instead of looking forward to the trip, I now saw it as a trial, an ordeal to be endured and got over with.

Why, I kept asking myself, did I feel so compelled to go? The only answer I could give was as flimsy as a dream. That dream of a perfect wave rising out of the polluted grey-green murk of the Venice lagoon; a wave I would never catch because of my hesitation over what to do with my wallet and keys. Like the opening paragraph of a novel that contains the germ of the whole tale, that dream – which had come to me on the eve of my return to the water – seemed to anticipate the host of contradictory feelings and tensions that my surfing odyssey would entail. The tension between the yearning for abandonment and the fear of losing control; between the domestic and the oceanic; between the secure pleasures of urban life and the savage pleasures of the surf; between Europe as the emblem of Western civilisation and Oceania as its 'barbarian' counterpart. Freud argues that all dreams are wish-fulfilments, and in my case, that was undoubtedly so. My compulsion to return to Europe came from the conviction that going there could somehow bring about the reconciliation of these apparently opposing worlds.

Not long before I left for Europe I was talking to Russell McConachy on the telephone. As always, we were moaning about the lack of swell. I was beginning to wonder whether I would ever get to see him surf at Two Mile Bay.

'I bet the surf picks up as soon as I go.'

'Given Murphy's Law, it probably will,' he said.

The swell arrived, as if on cue, the week I was due to leave but a last-minute dash down the coast was out of the question. With a million things to do before my departure, I might as well have been out of the country already. Jack kept me informed with rapturous email reports. Bells was corduroy, with clean, six-foot sets, polished to perfection by a stiff off-shore wind; and the swell was still rising. Two days later it hit ten foot. A huge crowd gathered on the cliffs at Bells and Winkipop to watch a handful of big wave surfers, including Russell, game enough to take it on. After two days of heart-in-the-mouth surfing, Jack was happy to stay on shore and gaze down the coast at the lines rolling in from the sea, every reef as far as the eye could see smoking and streaming great whitecaps in the wind.

I was glad for Jack and Russell and every other wave-starved surfer around, but I was too overwrought to be disappointed about missing out. When I told Jack about my fears, he gave a cryptic laugh. 'The boy'll be all right. Just draw a line in the sand around him and tell him not to go outside it. He'll be there when you get back.'

I sat on a bench outside Cambridge train station in the after-noon sunshine watching party-weary students tumbling from taxis and into the station on their way home for the summer. I felt surprisingly good. Now that it was fruitless to fret about my son, I had managed to jettison my fears and give myself up to the journey.

Fourteen years earlier, on my first trip to Europe, I'd come primed to step into the moody, black and white world of *The Third Man* or the grainy, dramatic footage of *The World at War*. The surf had no place in my film noir pastiche of the Old World; as I quickly discovered, neither did modern Europe. Even in Venice, which looked just as I'd expected, the parallel universe of the past constantly eluded me. Those massive, paint-flaked, arched doorways promised entry to that magical realm but they were always bolted. In flight from the youthful brashness of the New World (of which surfing was, in many ways, emblematic), I did not appreciate then that Europeans needed the Pacific to be their 'exotic' other, their ocean of desire, just as Australians needed Europe to be their fantasy past.

Andy Martin had once boldly described himself as the best surfer in Cambridge. As a boy growing up in East London, he had a recurring dream about a freak tidal wave that would come sweeping up the Thames and swamp the city. His parents, friends, brothers and teachers would be swept away, but he would survive by leaping onto a passing door or tree trunk and riding the crest of the gigantic wave to safety. As unlikely as such a wave might be, the tidal wave (as opposed to the tsunami) is not an unknown phenomenon in Britain. The Severn Bore, fed by the Bristol Channel, is the longest wave in Britain and one of the longest surfable waves in the world. On certain spring tides, usually at the equinox and just after a full and new moon, a wave of variable size is channelled into the River Severn and roars upstream for many miles. Andy now fantasised about the day when an even bigger wave would come roaring up the Cam. It was his opinion that the university, where he lectured in French, could be much improved if certain colleges were to be permanently submerged.

We were sitting in the courtyard of a bistro surrounded by Greek columns dripping creeper. Andy was very fair, with pink skin and white David Bowie hair. As he talked, I was trying to imagine a giant wave surging up the street towards us, but the surf felt too remote. 'Everything about surfing is rather subtle and verging on the metaphysical, or at least psychological,' Andy was saying. 'Except for the sheer size of a big wave. That's irrefutable.'

In his book *Walking on Water*, about big wave surfing in Hawaii, Andy happily cast himself as the pale, slightly nerdy academic, hopelessly out of his depth in the man-eating Hawaiian waves. My constant fear when reading the book was that he would suddenly prove himself otherwise.

Andy came to surfing relatively late. He was almost thirty when, on his way to a lecture tour of Australia and the States, he stopped in Bali. At Uluwatu, a place which felt to him like the end of the world, he witnessed surfing for the first time and was smitten. Recalling that experience now, he compared it to falling in love with a foreign language without being able to speak or understand it.

That surfing should appeal to Andy because it was redolent of a far-flung and exotic part of the world was, it struck me, a very European reaction. In Australia, surfing had been so successfully transplanted that it felt like an indigenous activity. Andy's first encounter with surfing placed him firmly within the tradition of European explorers' encounters with the Pacific, something of which he was very conscious. Surfing was all about the thrill of newness, of everything being 'radically other'.

At a table nearby some students were announcing that they had been up all night. I wondered where they would go for their holidays, now their exams were over. What did they do for their thrills, their taste of 'the other'?

Unlike many academics of post-colonial Pacific history who looked at the impact of imperialism on native peoples, Andy was more interested in the way Polynesian culture had 'colonised' the imagination of the Western world. He was writing a book on the explorer Comte Louis Antoine de Bougainville who, in 1768, claimed Tahiti for the French, describing it as a garden of Eden where Venus was the goddess of hospitality. Andy saw Bougainville's account of his voyage, which was published before Cook's journals of his Pacific explorations, as one of the earliest 'tourist brochures' for the South Pacific. *Voyage autour du monde* set out the charms of Tahiti and was responsible for disseminating two key myths: that there was no such thing as private property in Tahiti, and that everybody there was happy all the time. Thus, concluded Andy, Tahiti became Exhibit A in the case for the French revolution.

The glass conservatory roof over the bistro courtyard had turned it into an echo chamber and Andy had to speak up to make himself heard. It was fortunate, given the state of my jet-lagged brain, that he was happy to take an idea and run with it, with minimal prompting from his interlocutor. Clearly experienced in the art of lecturing over a din, he launched into his theory.

'It was the French who propagated the idea of paradise most powerfully at the end of the eighteenth century. The concept of happiness was very important in the French revolution. Happiness, *le bonheur*, was a universal human right for the revolutionaries. Reports about Tahiti, and Bougainville's book about his expedition gave the idea of paradise substance. Before that, people had utopias coming out their ears but no one had evidence of the existence of paradise. Then sailors came back from Tahiti and said, "It's actually out there." The French thought, "Well, if they can eat all the time and make love constantly and go surfing when they feel like it, how come we're living a life of suffering and misery?" This, to my way of thinking, underlay the French revolution.'

I grinned. *This* was what I had come to Cambridge for.

Expanding on this theory in his essay 'History of the Holiday', Andy notes that revolutionary ideology managed to gloss over the awkward fact that eighteenth-century France was nothing like Tahiti. In a characteristically droll twist, he evokes the Marquis de Sade, holed up in the Bastille reading Bougainville, as 'the shadowy behind-bars cheerleader of the whole operation. Not only did he take the idea of going *sans culotte* completely literally, his basic theory of the maximum pleasure to the point of pain, terror and death became the standard revolutionary manual for the next couple of centuries.' One might add that de Sade's theory about pleasure to the point of pain and death might well underlie the philosophy of the average big wave surfer; sadomasochism and big wave surfing have much in common.

I liked the way that even the most esoteric of Andy's interests, such as his book *The Knowledge of Ignorance*, always seemed to bring him back to surfing.

'I was trying to rectify the concept that knowledge is always a good thing. Many serious thinkers actually see ignorance as being positive, almost to the point of ignorance being some-thing unattainable, an ideal, mythic state that you could strive towards.'

'Something you strive towards?'

'It's a slightly perverse concept, the opposite of epistemology. Anepistemology they call it. I suppose surfing is an example of that impulse, that Rousseauesque drive to get away from culture.'

'The surfer as noble savage?' I suggested.

'Well, yes,' Andy smiled briefly. 'Except that you are never going to escape culture. Perhaps that's why we have this idealised image of the sole surfer on his or her own roaming the planet without anyone else around. But as soon as you've got more than one person on a beach, you've got a culture, even if it's beach culture. I've found that the same desires and fears and phobias and fantasies that you have on land are exacerbated when transposed to the water. You don't transcend anything. It's not like being on another planet or plane or realm. It's just a mirror image of society.'

I couldn't let that pass. It was true that the social dynamics of a crowded surf break could be medieval, even pre-historic. The best and most aggressive surfers dominated the waves and everyone else had to make do with what was left. And often, because of the size of the surf, the weather conditions or the surf break itself, you were more likely to feel frustrated and out of your depth than in perfect harmony with nature. But it wasn't always like that.

'When the waves aren't crowded, when the conditions are good, don't you think the ocean *can* feel like another world? And strangely, at the same time, like the place where you are most yourself, the place where you belong . . . ?' I trailed off, unable to adequately explain what I felt.

Andy looked dubious but was prepared to speculate. 'I think there are those moments when one has a sense of transcendence, maybe. Moments in which the ego is vanquished and you experience the self dissolving in a collective oneness. Maybe *that* is the oceanic feeling. But I feel you need to see those moments in a larger context. Most of the time you're at two with nature, not one.'

It was six months since his last surf and Andy was given to grumbling about life in Cambridge. 'I mean, look at this place,' he exclaimed in a cultured drawl. 'My God, how much surfing can you get done here?' But for all that, he had come to the conclusion that being deprived of the surf for long periods ensured that it remained a special and even miraculous experience. 'I ask myself the slightly cynical question, "If I were free to surf on a full time basis, would the love die?" I hesitate to answer it.'

At first sight, Newquay, spread along high cliffs overlooking the surf, reminded me momentarily of Bondi, although it lacked Bondi's decadent glamour. I had been warned that while Newquay was undoubtedly the surf centre of Britain, it was 'full of lager louts and would-be surfers'. On the plane from Bangkok to London, I had found myself next to a young engineer from Warwick who said he was going to Newquay to celebrate a friend's bucks party in a few weeks time. Things were starting to sound ominous.

Trying to get my bearings, I followed the main street, past games parlours with flashing light bulbs, brightly painted surf shops with racks of boards out the front, and rambling, run-down hotels. Where the shops ended there was a cliff top promenade with public benches overlooking the water. Here, many elderly people were gathered with their walking sticks gazing out to sea or strolling slowly along the path.

Leaning on the fence, I looked down and was surprised to see parallel lines of swell rolling in from the North Atlantic, gradually warping to accommodate the curve of shapely Newquay Bay before breaking in snappy, three-foot waves not unlike those I was used to catching at Jan Juc. On the way into town I'd briefly caught sight of the water and thought, 'No surf today.' It had been easy enough not to have any expectations of the Cornish surf. If the north shore of Hawaii could be dead flat in winter when it ought to be at its biggest, then it seemed foolish to expect much of the Cornish coast in summer.

Beneath my initial disappointment about the apparent lack of surf, there lurked a sneaking satisfaction. When a young Australian surfer chose to study Surf Science and Technology at Plymouth University, his decision was considered worthy of an article in the *Age* and the *Sydney Morning Herald*. You could almost see the smirk on the journalist's face as she observed, '[England's] cold, there's not much surf and, let's face it, the idea of the umbrella-wielding English teaching suntanned Australians how to master waves seems a bit odd.' As crude as I found her national stereotypes, I couldn't pretend that

I didn't share some of that journalist's bemusement, her sense of the incongruity. Not only was surfing one of the few pursuits that Australia had introduced to Britain, it was one of the few pursuits in which Australia could assume the kind of superiority that Britain had for so long assumed over its colonial outpost.

I had grown up with an Anglophile father who had never been overseas but who subscribed to magazines like *Country Life* and *This England*, and who harboured a secret longing to be an English country gentleman. I thought him hopelessly nostalgic. Although I was twenty-five when I first went to Britain, I reacted to the place like a rebellious adolescent, sitting in disdainful judgement on everything I saw and heard. How tame those green hills looked. How posh and twittering British voices sounded. I had come in search of the past, and yet almost every reminder of it, from the Tower of London to King's College, made me bristle. While I would have happily succumbed to the tourist cliché of a gondola in Venice, I went punting on the Cam with great reluctance, fearful that I might find myself aping those foppish types from *Brideshead Revisited*.

Fourteen years on, having been back here a number of times, I no longer took the historical relationship between Australia and Britain so personally. So why was I so ready to assume that there wouldn't be 'real' surf in Cornwall? Why did I feel that there was something inexpressibly strange, something uncanny, about the sight of people in wetsuits walking the streets of a Cornish town? With the eye of the coloniser,

I found myself smiling on the efforts of the natives to model their conduct, dress and lingo on that of their conquerors.

It didn't seem to matter that, strictly speaking, the surf culture Australia exported to Britain was not of its own making but an antipodean off-shoot of the Californian beach cult. In the early 1960s, a group of Australian lifesavers came to Newquay and other Cornish coastal towns to work on the beaches during the northern summer. They brought with them the nine-foot foam and fibreglass malibu boards that had revolutionised Australian surfing half a decade earlier when introduced by American lifeguards. Those were the basic facts about the origins of modern surfing in Britain. But ultimately I was not grappling with facts. I was grappling with historical baggage and national myths.

I found a room in a large, faded-looking Edwardian hotel. The best thing about it was that it was opposite Tolcarne Beach; to go for a surf, all I had to do was whack on my wetsuit and cross the road.

I asked the woman at the reception desk whether she would mind if I took the board I had hired into my room.

'That's fine,' she smiled. 'It's either surfboards or wheel-chairs today.' The hotel, like many others along the Padstow road, was occupied by big groups of elderly citizens on coach tours.

I bought a Cornish pastie and found a seat overlooking Towan Beach, at the opposite end of the town, with a view of the whole of Newquay Bay. The wind had dropped and the waves were much glassier than before. At around a quarter to nine in the evening on summer nights at home, the sun would be disappearing behind the horizon and night would be starting to fall. Dusk in Australia was always a relatively short interlude before the curtain came down. For this reason, and because of the danger posed by sharks, you didn't see many Australian surfers in the water in the evenings. I'd forgotten about these lingering northern twilights, and was astounded to count almost a hundred surfers in the water between Towan and Lusty Glaze at the far end of the bay.

That night I listened to the mewling of the gulls nesting outside my window, a sound I had earlier mistaken for a kitten trapped on the roof. The melancholy, drawn-out cry of these northern gulls was nothing like the raucous squawk of the silver gulls that scavenged on Australian beaches. At the same time, it was hauntingly familiar. It was the sound of the phantom seaside I had known all my life; the seaside of British radio, television and film; the seaside I had not seen until now and yet knew as intimately as I knew Arnold's Dover Beach or Coleridge's painted ocean.

At low tide the next morning the beach was three times the width it had been the night before. Australian tides retreat a few metres at most; here, it was as if the vast, rippled underbelly of the sea had been rudely stripped of its covering; left naked, quivering and exposed. Later, I would dream about going down to the beach for a surf only to find that the tide had retreated so far out that the sea had disappeared from the horizon, possibly never to return.

Like many coastal towns, Newquay embraced the most protected tracts of water and turned its back on the wildest part of the coast. With the town still asleep, I took the road to Towan Head – the headland at the western end of the bay – which also led to Britain's version of Bells Beach and its best known surfing arena, Fistral Bay. Unlike Newquay Bay, Fistral was not protected by high cliffs. Behind it lay a large, featureless golf course which rendered the whole foreshore bald and barren. The surf was definitely bigger here, but the waves were wind blown and raw. In fact, the beauty of the place lay in its rawness, its faint air of neglect – a quality that was soon to be threatened by a council decision to sell the beach to a private development company. Newquay locals were understandably worried about the changes this sale would bring, and whether charges might restrict public access to the beach. The concept of an individual, family or business *owning* a beach was not alien to them, however. Two of the beaches in Newquay Bay were privately owned.

In Australia, all beaches are public property. I had always thought of the beach as something that could not be owned, could not be bought or sold. A beach was, in my mind, one of the very few scraps of landscape left on earth immune to the voracious logic of capitalism. The beach belonged to everybody.

St Agnes, a typical Cornish village, offered a perfect contrast to Newquay. It was all stone miners' cottages, low-roofed taverns, shady, narrow lanes, and foxgloves and wild roses spilling out from the roadside. The chimneys of engine houses left over from the days of tin mining were scattered like sentinels over the surrounding hills. A short walk from the town lay a pretty little cove with bathing boxes and colourful, upturned boats on the sand. One of the oldest surfers in the village was a woman called Ginger, who went in every day of the year, without a wetsuit, on her original Cornish surfboard – a small, laminated wooden precursor of the body board. Perhaps a Cornish sailor on one of Cook's or Bligh's voyages brought back the idea from Tahiti or Hawaii.

It was Peter Lascelles who pointed Ginger out as she puttered back from the beach in a well-preserved Morris Minor. As the owner of the only surfing business in the village, Peter was St Agnes's surfing overlord. We sat in the sun at a table in front of The Tap House, at the lower end of the village. Stocky and round-faced, Peter knew everyone who went past. This sense of community was what had drawn him to St Agnes from Queensland and what continued to keep him here over twenty years since he first visited Cornwall to work as a lifeguard.

I was finding it hard to reconcile the quaint, Old World village charm of St Agnes with the New World brazenness of surf culture. Peter said that surfing had taken over from rugby, cricket and football as the preferred sport of the young people in the village. That it should take over from cricket, of all games, seemed significant: the two were antithetical. Cricket was traditionally the game of gentlemen and regarded as a civilising force – especially in the colonies. Surfing was traditionally the chosen pursuit of youthful rebels who thrived on the elemental anarchy of the unpredictable ocean. 'Few things are more deeply rooted in the collective imagination of the English than the village cricket match,' writes Geoffrey Moorhouse. 'It stirs a romantic illusion about the rustic way of life, it suggests a tranquil and unchanging order in an age of bewildering flux, and it persuades a lot of townsfolk that that is where they would rather be.' Surfing, not cricket, was now more likely to persuade townsfolk that a coastal village was where they would rather be. That illusion of 'tranquil and unchanging order' could clearly not be sustained. Was this why surfing, with its promise of personal freedom, now resonated more deeply with the youth of Britain than the team spirit and gentlemanly values of cricket?

The popularity of surfing could be most obviously measured in its commercial success. Being a soul surfer at heart, I had shied away from surfing's mercantile side and done my best to ignore stories about drop-out surfers from the 1960s and 1970s who had gone on to establish multinational surfing empires. Newspaper articles on the subject, usually in the Business pages, read like postmodern fables about capitalism being the natural and inescapable order governing human affairs. If surfers, those radical outsiders who had once shunned mainstream existence and its materialistic values in favour of a simple life by the sea, could not resist the lure of the dollar, then why should anyone else try?

Peter had no illusions about the nature of the sell-out by surfers of his generation. 'You start out being a rebel, being anti the establishment and you end up smack where you didn't want to be. You end up being the person about whom twenty years ago you said, "I'm not going to be like him. He's got too much money, he's a capitalist." '

As far as I was concerned, the surf industry was a philistine, commercial juggernaut that had nothing to do with what surfing was really about. It traded on the oceanic mystique of surfing – the pure simplicity of a man or woman riding a wave – and the frontier mystique of the lifestyle, while transforming both into mainstream commodities. I liked to believe that no matter how commercial surfing became it could never impinge on the purity of one's experience in the water. But my unconscious must have had some doubts. In one of my now frequent dreams about surfing, I arrived at Jan Juc to find that a section of the beach was a gigantic shopfront. I had to fold back concertina-like French windows and then paddle around racks of t-shirts and wetsuits and surfboards to get out to the break. Because of all the merchandise, there was very little space in which to catch whatever tiny waves came my way. Apart from the horrible fact that big business had invaded the ocean itself, what bothered me most was the feeling of being closed in, of not being able to see in either direction up the coast. A few other surfers languidly hovered nearby like indifferent shop assistants, occasionally smirking at my efforts to catch a wave.

One of the things I admired about Jack Finlay was the way he had tried to stir up debate within the surfing community about the industry's domination of surf culture. He had written his story 'Fat City' out of a feeling that commercial interests were swamping the sport while the surfing press remained supine and unquestioning. Not surprisingly, he'd had trouble finding surfing publications that would air, let alone take up, the criticisms he felt needed to be made. The surf media had diversified considerably since the 1980s when Jack first tried to publicise his views, and recognising untapped markets, the industry had become more open to those groups it had previously shunned – women, older surfers, boogie boarders and general beachgoers. In fact, the industry had become so mainstream that one no longer needed to be a surfer to wear surf attire. Surfing as an image and the act of surfing had completely parted ways. The greatest sin in Jack's view was that the surf industry had made its wealth at the expense of surf culture; that it had rendered the surfing world a material-istic desert bereft of sophisticated ideas, artistic vision and intellectual debate.

Surfers like Jack and me were, however, in a minority. Even Andy Martin was inclined to take a more benign view of surfing's commercial side. He believed that an emphasis on appearance and salesmanship was integral to surfing from the beginning; that the ancient Hawaiian chanters who proclaimed the prowess of their chiefs were like their publicists. The phenomenon of soul surfing was, he argued, the aberration; the exception rather than the rule.

When Peter first came to Cornwall, there were four surf shops in Newquay. Now there were thirty-four. Newquay then had a population of about six thousand people; now it was twenty-five thousand. Surfing had transformed the town and was estimated to be worth forty million pounds annually to Cornwall's economy. Since wetsuits had made surfing possible all year round, and the boogie board had made surfing an affordable family pastime, the British had embraced beach culture with unprecedented fervour. It was Peter's opinion that they brought a more philosophical, jovial spirit to surfing than other nations because the conditions here were more trying. British surfers put up with weather that would keep surfers or beachgoers from more temperate climates indoors. Ginger was a perfect example.

Andy was slightly more cynical. An article he had once written about a trip to Hawaii had prompted a letter to the *Guardian* from 'Outraged of Newquay'. It went, he said, something like this: 'Andy Martin, who the bloody hell does he think he is, sodding off to Hawaii, blue skies, blue seas and the surf is up. Whereas true surfing is all about bobbing up and down on the water for hours on end with the waves completely shitty and the rain pissing down. That's true surfing.'

'I'm caricaturing a bit,' Andy conceded. 'But this slightly perverse, pain-orientated approach – the inverse of hedonism – is an integral part of British surfing. You get these occasional shreds and patches of pleasure but the core experience is deemed to be disappointment. Indeed, discontent. The pleasure principle is out there on someone else's planet, not this one.'

Peter urged me to see a black comedy about surfing that had been filmed in St Agnes called *Blue Juice*. 'It's a piss-take that shows up the silly side of surfing,' he said. Piss-taking was something the British were very good at, especially when the satire was directed at themselves. I had always assumed that the more macho and juvenile aspects of modern surf culture were a reflection of the frontier mentality of the New World countries that had spawned it, and I'd hoped that in British and French attitudes to surfing I would find a more sophisticated and satisfying balance of culture (in its broadest sense) and nature; youthful exuberance and mature reflection. While I had seen little sign of this so far, I thought that *Blue Juice* might provide insights into British surfing that I had missed.

As it turned out, there were plenty of insights – but not those the film intended. It is true that *Blue Juice* does have a dig at the Boys' Own, surf-or-die, commitment-phobic culture. But as an attempt at piss-taking, it completely fizzles out when the surfing hero, JC, saves his mate from the monster surf of the Boneyard and becomes a model dad. More Carry on Surfing than satire, the film inadvertently reveals how monolithic surf culture has become. The Cornish village atmosphere, the country lanes and the British accents are among the few features of the film that give it a regional flavour. Everything else – the fashions, the laddish behaviour, the single-minded pursuit of the waves, the fear of growing up, the surfing heroics – are case book features of global surf culture that the British have imported, so it seems, without modification. Without a hint of irony.

That evening the surf at St Agnes was mushy and little more than an occasional surge. The compensation, though, was the setting – the craggy, grass-topped granite cliffs, the engine house chimneys, the intimate cove with its sand and pebble beach. Soon the sun disappeared behind the high cliffs. A slick, blue-black head popped up out of the water nearby. For a moment it looked almost human, then I thought it was a dog out for a swim. For a short time the seal swam around amongst us, as if in want of company, then it dove beneath the surface with the flick of its fan-like tail. A chill was settling over the water and although the surf was showing no sign of improving, a small number of surfers were still making the most of what was on offer. Unable to stand the cold any longer, I headed in. Even as I made my way back to the car in the fading light, more surfers were arriving at the beach still hopeful for a wave or, perhaps, as Andy and Peter had suggested, simply for the pleasure of getting wet.

In bed, after dinner at the pub around the corner where every conversation in the bar seemed to contain a whisper of the surf, I read a slim volume of Cornish legends. There were stories of giants, mermaids and witches, but the only one that lodged in my mind was a brief, haunting fragment called 'The Voice From the Sea'. It told of a fisherman walking along the sand one night at Porthtowan, the long beach just outside St Agnes. Above the surge and fall of the waves, the fisherman heard a voice coming from the sea: 'The hour is come, but not the man.' After this had been repeated three times, a black figure like that of a man appeared at the top of the hill, paused for a moment, then rushed down the steep slope, across the beach and into the sea. What this dream-like tale was supposed to signify, I had no idea. Yet the underlying mood of terror and compulsion that drove the man headlong into the water, as if answering an irresistible call, was all too familiar.

For the first twelve years of her life, Virginia Woolf spent her summers at St Ives. The harbour town was one of her most beloved places and the source of some of her happiest memories. The Stephen family stopped going to St Ives after the death of Woolf's mother, Julia, thus preserving the town in Woolf's memory as the childhood idyll she had inhabited before tragedy struck and mental illness descended. Although her novel *To the Lighthouse* is set on a Hebridian island, it was inspired by Woolf's summers in Cornwall and her return to St Ives eleven years after her mother's death. Since taking up surfing again, I had returned to Woolf's writing and been surprised by the extent to which ocean waves – actual and metaphorical – pulsate through her writing. Being in Cornwall now gave me the chance to see where Woolf had spent those golden summers and to witness the waves that imprinted themselves on her work.

In her novel *The Waves* Woolf 'tried to walk on water', writes Jeanette Winterson, so that her readers might too. It's an audacious, disturbing image, given that Woolf died by drowning. 'She wanted to write about the vast unknown uncertain continent that is the world and us in it. This continent is not a land mass. It is not solid, it is not stable.

It shifts, it storms, it drowns, it is both the simple surface of things and their depths.' What *The Waves* offers, it seemed to me, is a kind of psychological surfing on wave after wave of six friends' thoughts and reflections, from childhood through to old age, each wave distinct yet intermingling with the next. Running throughout the characters' intense, silent soliloquies is a preoccupation with both their separateness from each other and their sense of oneness. They see themselves as a series of waves that travel through life together only to 'burst asunder' upon the shore.

St Ives has a long history as a fishing port and, more recently, as an artists' colony. A coastal resort which oozes gentrified charm and quaintness, not to mention the trappings of high culture, it seemed, on the surface, a far cry from scrubby, unsophisticated Newquay. Instead of cheek-by-jowl surf shops full of equipment with which to *engage* with the sea, the narrow lanes behind the St Ives harbourfront are chocked up with commercial galleries full of marine images and seascapes – a thousand different ways of *seeing* the sea. In the end, though, both towns are flogging their respective sea cultures in a quest for the tourist dollar, both capitalising on their assets: St Ives on its artistic heritage as the home of the *plein air* painters in the nineteenth century and the St Ives School of abstract painting in the mid-twentieth century; Newquay on its fine beaches and surf.

It was a relief to escape the art-laden lanes for the open, sandy expanse of Porthmeor Beach. Families huddled behind windbreaks, only the children game enough to brave the stiff wind and dash into the water. Occasional, promising lines of swell rolled into the bay but, battered by the on-shore wind, most failed to take shape as rideable waves. I watched two surfers on long boards chasing whatever sluggish surges materialised but felt no inclination to rush back to the carpark to grab my board. These were waves for thinking, not surfing, on.

Woolf writes of waves breaking with 'muffled thuds, like logs falling, on the shore'. Sometimes her waves are mesmerising patterns of water lit up by sunshine, splintering like glass or sweeping a quick fan over the beach. But more often than not, her waves are metaphors for powerful surges of emotion, such as fear of annihilation, of going under to madness, of flux, chaos and instability. Her waves can evoke daily rhythms, or life at its most intense, the pure, unforgettable moment. Yet there is no mystical merging of civilisation and nature for Woolf. *The Waves*, she writes, must show 'that effort, effort, dominates: not the waves'.

In the second part of *To the Lighthouse*, when all the vibrant chatter and argument fade away, when deaths are relegated to terse sentences in parentheses, the narrator ponders whether old sources of consolation, such as walking along the beach and contemplating the sea, can still provide solace.

'Did nature supplement what man advanced? Did she complete what he began? With equal complacency she saw his misery, condoned his meanness, and acquiesced in his torture. That dream, then, of sharing, completing, finding in solitude on the beach an answer, was but a reflection in a mirror, and the mirror itself was but the surface glassiness which forms in quiescence when the nobler powers sleep beneath?'

I too had come here with that dream 'of sharing, completing, finding in solitude on the beach an answer'; of finding that elusive, impossible blend of history, culture and nature. Halfway along the beach I looked up at the houses on the hill and saw a great, bone-white building like an avant-garde ocean liner nosing its way towards the water. This, I discovered, was the Tate Gallery. The cry of gulls and the yelps of the children playing on the beach faded as I entered the unnatural hush of the foyer. Here was a moodier St Ives than the one I had just walked through. Here was *Beach at Dusk, St Ives Harbour*, all mellow and impressionistic in evening greens, painted by William Osborn, an early member of the St Ives Arts Club. Here was Alfred Wallis's *Wreck of the Alba*, a stylised, naive depiction of the fate of the SS *Alba*, which ran aground in heavy seas on Porthmeor Beach in 1938. That very beach lay just outside the building, yet the images contained in this dimly lit room belonged to another world. Having transformed the real world, they were no longer of it. Some vital connection had been severed.

I was trying to make sense of Ian Hamilton's cryptic maritime works – stones inscribed with words such as 'WAVE' in large letters, playful postcards punning on maritime themes – when I heard a woman behind me say, 'Wonderful view!' I turned to see a semi-circular window like an amphitheatre that formed a light-filled frame for the sea beyond. In the far right corner I could just see a surfer on a red board. The rest was shifting shades of blue. It was, without doubt, the most mesmerising image in the gallery. For a few moments I could not take my eyes off the moving, luminous water beyond the glass. The sea appeared to surge into the gallery and the gallery to embrace the sea. How seductive it was, this illusion that nature and art are not divided, that one flows into the other and out again. It seemed a kind of enchantment; but as soon as I stepped outside the gallery, the spell was broken. The gallery looked bereft and empty. The sea was just the sea.

If there was a work missing from the Tate Gallery's maritime collection it was the picture Lily Briscoe paints in the final pages of *To the Lighthouse*. While Mr Ramsay and his children make their pilgrimage to the lighthouse, Lily does combat with her blank canvas. This final section of the novel shifts back and forward between two perspectives: Lily in the garden looking out over the sea, and the Ramsay children in their little yacht amid the tossing waves, 'a log wallowing down one wave; a gull riding another'. Lily, it seems, is the observer-artist, always standing at the edge of things. The Ramsays are active participants immersed in life – they are literally in the picture Lily is painting.

This distinction, this matter of perspective, was one I was constantly grappling with as I wrote this book: how to be 'in the picture' and make the picture at the same time; how to find a balance between surfing and writing. Like Lily, I often asked myself why art had to draw one away from ordinary life.

Yet as Lily fills her canvas with blues and greens, she too goes on a journey as vivid and real and disturbing as that made by the Ramsays in their boat. Tellingly, Woolf describes the experience as being 'down in the hollow of one wave' and seeing 'the next towering higher and higher above her'. Immersed in her painting, Lily is drawn down into herself to the point where she loses consciousness of the outer world. Yet this inward, artistic process is described by Woolf as being like a journey towards the horizon: 'Out and out one went, further and further, until at last one seemed to be on a narrow plank, perfectly alone, over the sea.' And when Lily finally resurfaces from the depths of her painting, as if emerging from the surf, she brings with her the revelation that only words and paint can defy the passing of time, the constant flux of the universe. In the end, that is the only difference between art and life.

On the way to the carpark, I passed the St Ives Arts Club, a distinctive stone building with a dark-stained, upper storey of wood smack up against the harbour. In a book in the Tate, I had seen a photograph of the club being battered and almost engulfed by a giant wave during a storm in 1991. One hundred years earlier, the wooden upper storey had been swept away by a similar storm which brought tremendous seas into the bay. An onlooker reported seeing a considerable portion of the Arts Club floating around the headland. Surreal and chaotic, it was the kind of 'performance art' that only nature can pull off, a perfect image of the disintegration and flux that Lily Briscoe was trying to arrest.

I returned to Newquay feeling flat and Sunday afternoon-ish. The following morning I had to head back to London, my

Cornish excursion over. I'd given up all hope of getting a surf before I left; it was sad, but there was nothing to be done about it. At Tolcarne Beach I glanced, without expectation, at the bay. The surf at St Agnes and St Ives had been blown out by a cross-shore wind but here, to my delight and surprise, the high cliffs protected the bay sufficiently for the waves to be shapely and clean.

Half an hour later I was making my way down the steep path to Great Western Beach, my bare feet welcoming the hard warmth of the concrete. The sun was out, the sea was an improbable jade. And, amazingly, there was hardly anyone in the water. After a restless day of touring and thinking, of being the eternal onlooker, immersion was bliss. I paddled for a nice little right-hander. At first it seemed that I wouldn't make it, but with a few extra strokes came that exquisite moment of freefall when you slip into a kind of still point and watch the world rush by. Gliding down the open face of the wave, I reached out my hand to steady myself against its shimmering, hollow belly. I watched my fingers trace a foaming white arc. Every time this happened it thrilled me, the intimacy of the act, as if I was caressing the tender inside of a lover's thigh. The waves kept coming. Next time it was a left-hander with a nice round shoulder on which to hover before swooping to its base, turning and floating over the back of the wave as it collapsed into foam. For once, I lost count of the waves that I caught. During a lull between sets, I looked up at the purple cliffs topped with a soft fuzz of grass, at the buildings flowing up the hill beyond, and the melancholy gulls hovering above the rooftops, and felt a sudden surge of affection. When you were in the water, Newquay was not such a bad place to be.

The Bassin d'Arcachon forms the only break in the two hundred and thirty kilometres of beach known as the Côte d'Argent that stretches from the Gironde estuary, just north of Bordeaux, to Bayonne near the Spanish border. South of Bayonne lies the Basque coast, the cradle of surfing in Europe. In the surfing world, if not beyond it, the Côte d'Argent is famed for its powerful beach breaks, while the Basque coast is prized for its many point and reef breaks, which can hold Hawaiian-sized waves. The English might have trumped the French in the race to colonise the Pacific, but Britain can never hope to rival France's geographical edge when it comes to surf.

Since first landing in Paris on Bastille Day in 1988, I had been as infatuated with France as I was ambivalent about Britain. There were no oedipal tensions to mar this relationship, and I knew that if I ever had the opportunity to live outside Australia, France would be my first choice. In fact, my partner and I were seriously considering the idea of spending at least six months here the following year. Surely if any nation could combine the best of civilisation with the best of surfing, it had to be the French.

Despite having made six journeys to France over the years, I had never been to the Atlantic coast. Most Australians visit

France for its culture, its history, its romance, its food and wine, its gloriously varied countryside – not for beaches or surf. My only experience of the French coastline was the decayed, world-weary splendour of the Riviera.

A few months earlier, in the film *Sous le Sable*, I had seen the Atlantic coast for the first time. A Parisian couple visit their holiday house near the small town of Lit et Mixe on the south-west coast one weekend. To get to the beach they walk through a dark forest of pine trees and emerge onto an empty stretch of wild beach pounded by heavy surf. The woman lies on the sand to read; her husband, a big, sleepy bear of a man, walks into the waves and never returns. Later in Paris, the woman is lecturing on Woolf's *The Waves* when, overcome by grief and the memories stirred by the novel, she breaks down.

As I drove through similar pine forests, I thought of the film and its landscape and how there had been a rush on *The Waves* at Melbourne bookshops when *Sous le Sable* was screening. Preoccupied, I missed the Arcachon turn-off. The occasional, secluded villa began appearing amid the trees and a sign announced that I had arrived in Cap Ferret. This sparsely populated holiday hamlet was at the end of the narrow peninsula that forms the northern side of the bay. Eating oysters at a restaurant overlooking the Bassin that evening, I could see the lights of Arcachon blinking across the water.

It was a weekend in late June, the summer solstice, and yet it felt like off-season, reminding me of a remote, windswept

Greek island I had once visited which seemed to be eternally waiting for tourists who never arrived. Fifty years ago, before the road was built, Cap Ferret was accessible only by boat, its inhabitants either fishermen or oyster farmers. It wasn't until wealthy Parisians started building their holiday villas amid the pines that it grew into something resembling a village. Some of the oldest man-made features were the concrete World War II bunkers on the beach which were now covered with surfing graffiti.

I found a room in a hotel that faced the high dunes of the Atlantic coast. To the south lay the *passes*, the treacherous narrows of the basin, to the north an infinity of white-gold sand. This wealth, this surfeit, of sand had been a powerful brake on human habitation of the region, as had the porous nature of the rock beneath the surface which transformed the coastal hinterland into a swamp during the winter months. Only when the shifting sands were stabilised by vast plantations of pine and the land drained in the nineteenth century did the area become more settled. But the region remained underpopulated and this sparsely settled quality, in conjunction with the instability of the landscape, gave it more of a frontier atmosphere than anywhere else I had been in France.

It was not surprising, then, that surfing came late to Cap Ferret – in the 1970s, almost twenty years after Biarritz. One of the first surfers here was Patrick Lataste. He had lived in America and travelled the world but had come back here because this was *his* heart's coast. A sinewy man in his late forties, he told me that his parents were horrified when he took up surfing, having always thought of the ocean as a place of danger and death. In 1836, a disaster that claimed the lives of many fishermen and became known as the Great Sorrow had etched itself into the psyche of the inhabitants of the Bassin and persisted in the collective memory of subsequent generations. Traditional beliefs in the region held that waves were the souls of drowned men without tombs. They were obliged to tow the white wash up to the water's edge for all eternity unless the wife or daughter of the drowned man recognised the wave at her feet and said a prayer for his soul.

One could surf the *passes* on the right tide and in the right weather conditions, but because the waves broke on sand bars distant from the shore, it was necessary – as at Corsair – to take a boat to the break. Although Patrick had made it his 'project' to surf there, his two attempts to do so had had to be abandoned because he had misjudged the tides. Even Patrick's friends who were experienced fishermen, feared the place. In fact, fishermen had been the first to surf the break, Patrick said. 'They go out when it's really big and surf their boats to make it back in.'

'It's a pretty fickle place, Cap Ferret. You have to have a lot of patience to surf here. We can have exquisite quality but not as often as somewhere like Hossegor. But then Hossegor is full of people.'

I had the feeling that I was overhearing a conversation that Patrick often had with himself, as if he still wondered about the wisdom of having returned.

In the dunes behind the empty, windswept beach near the

passes, a man was setting up a makeshift cafe of yellow plastic tables and chairs which he would later dismantle. It was hard to imagine enough people appearing in Cap Ferret to make his effort worthwhile.

Hossegor might mean little to most international tourists, but to the surfing cognoscenti, it is the epicentre of France. Its powerful, hollow beach breaks are widely regarded as among the best in the world. And there was no mistaking that Hossegor, like Newquay, is a surf company town. Large, colourful surf emporiums dominated the main shopping strip, while surf factories the size of aircraft hangars dominated the nearby industrial estate. As with most of the resorts along the Côte d'Argent, there were very few old churches or build-ings of historical or cultural value; although for those with more pagan instincts who worshipped at the altar of the sea, there was the promise of liquid cathedrals. Having always loved Debussy's limpid, watery music, especially the hollow, ringing procession of chords in his piano prelude 'The Sunken Cathedral', I had come to France with a ready-made sound-track for the surf. All that was required were the waves.

I found the perfect venue for wave-watching – a hotel room that faced onto one of the best surf breaks on the main beach. The balcony was like an exclusive box at the opera. How perfect! Except that the curtain never went up. A haze of low, gauzy cloud hung over the town for the next two days, swept in by an on-shore wind which messed the small swell into dispiriting little hummocks of grey and white. *The essence of*

any surf journey is not the surf but the possibility of it, was the
Zen-like entry in my journal that night.

South of Hossegor, close to the Spanish border, lay Biarritz and
the Basque coast; a very different world from the vast wilderness of beach I had seen so far. Here, just outside Biarritz, was
Guéthary, a village of neat, white-wash and red timber houses
on a hill overlooking a sea that boasted Europe's biggest surf.
It was an ancient whaling and fishing port. The world's first
commercial whalers, the Basques had built stone whale-
spotting towers along the coast, one of which remains at
Guéthary. 'Many say that the first to take on this harrowing
adventure must have been fanatic – eccentrics and dare-devils.
It would not have begun, they say, with reasonable Nordics,
but only with the Basques, those giddy adventurers,' observes
Jules Michelet in *La Mer*. Michelet was writing about whaling,
but he might well have been describing those who first dared
to surf the whale-sized waves that can fetch up on the reefs
here.

This time my hotel room had no view of the water. But in
the dining room hung a large photograph of a giant wave
crashing against an apartment block that sits right on the
Guéthary waterfront; it reminded me of the wave I'd seen
assaulting the St Ives Arts Club. The Guéthary photo, taken
during a famous storm in 1959, before a breakwater was built
in front of the apartments, caught the wave in the moment of
collision as it exploded in jets of white spray that reached the
upper floors of the building. It was no wonder that houses in

the region were traditionally built with their backs to the sea. Guéthary's biggest waves, however, broke on reefs up to a kilometre from the shore. Unlike the extended continental shelf around Britain, the Iberian shelf was narrow and dropped off steeply close to shore. The full force of the Atlantic, driven into this sharp corner where France and Spain meet, was sent skyward when it hit the outlying reefs – known to surfers as Parlementia and Avalanche.

Surfing first penetrated French consciousness as an *idea* which was then put into practice – as opposed to being demonstrated by visiting surfers, as happened elsewhere. According to the Americans James Houston and Ben Finney, swimming enthusiasts near Bayonne first read about the sport and heard tales of its glamour and excitement. 'After examining published plans of surf boards and studying technique in books, they built their own boards and proceeded to teach themselves.' In the French version of this history, it was surfing footage in a documentary about the bombing of Pearl Harbor that inspired a French body boarder to try his hand at building a stand-up board. (The traditional French body board, a wooden plank with a scoop at the front called a *planky*, is akin to the traditional Cornish body board.) But lack of knowledge about the need to wax the surface of a board for traction scuttled these early attempts. Then, in 1956, the American screenwriter Peter Viertel, who had seen surfing in California but had never surfed himself, and a Frenchman Georges Hennebutte, who was adept at riding the *planky*, became the first men to walk on French waves.

This story appealed to me because it captured an important cultural difference between the empirically inclined Anglo-Saxons and the more theoretically inclined French; a cultural predisposition that seemed to make the French much more susceptible to the *idea of surfing* – surfing as metaphor. This was brought home to me when I read the blurb on the French translation of my first novel: '*Night Surfing* describes a universe of solitude and wandering, of characters washed up in sublime and haunting landscapes. In this book, the ocean opens up and closes down. Symbolic, frightening, monstrous, abyss or womb, it gives a metaphysical dimension to surfing far removed from Californian imagery.' That the publishers should stress the difference between surfing as a form of philosophical engagement and surfing as an expression of American popular culture was, it seemed to me, a quintessentially French thing to do.

Behind the apartments on the waterfront was a wide viewing platform with pitted, grey concrete balustrades. I stood with Gibus de Soultrait looking out over the Bay of Biscay.

'I learned how to surf at the beach just below here,' he said.

The low, gauzy cloud was finally starting to clear but there was no surf to be seen. The water was wind-ruffled but waveless.

We stared down at an ugly slick of foam, plastic bags and bottles, logs and other muck that hugged the shoreline beneath the village. The daily appearance of this slick had inspired Gibus to help form the European chapter of the Surfrider Foundation. For years the Foundation had waged a campaign against the dumping of raw garbage.

'I saw a bulldozer last night cleaning the beach,' I said.

'They do that every day. We are putting pressure on the politicians. But there is a long way to go.'

Nearby, a group of young surfers with skateboards were hanging about, waiting for some action. They greeted Gibus warmly. Although he was only in his mid-forties, he was one of the village's big wave pioneers and seemed to command respect. He lived in a large house on the cliffs overlooking the water and, as his name suggested, he came from an aristocratic family. I knew from speaking to other local surfers that Gibus had a strong sense of *noblesse oblige*. He had helped younger surfers to build up their confidence in big waves and he believed that older surfers had a responsibility to live up to their 'past dream'.

Gibus pointed out toward the hidden reefs that produced Guéthary's famous big waves. For all his evident passion for the surf, he spoke of it with philosophical detachment. Even the way he dressed – smart baggy pants and a loose, striped shirt, combined with bookish, dark-rimmed spectacles – reinforced his air of composure. I imagined him paddling into a wave with perfect *sang froid*.

'When the waves are really big – eighteen or twenty foot – it looks like there's an island out on the horizon. It goes black. From the shore you don't realise the size. It's always something else when you reach the line-up because of the noise, the power, the size of the waves. The waves have their own will, so the first thing you learn is the experience of humility.'

Certain waves were fixed in his memory – his surfing 'spots

of time'. One day he launched into a fifteen-foot wave and flew down the glassy slope in a stomach-churning swoop to find a huge spinning barrel opening up before him. As he entered the gigantic, deep-green cavern he knew that he might not reach the end before it collapsed. For a few endless seconds, he inhabited that vast liquid tunnel. Then the lens of the wave contracted, the blue sky at the far end disappeared and the world imploded. A friend, who had filmed his ride, showed the footage at a surf screening that evening. 'Suddenly I saw my wave, which was so strong inside me, up there on the huge screen.'

If I had tried to dream up a surfer to embody the French *ésprit de surfing*, I could not have improved on Gibus. He had established the first European surfing magazine, *Surf Session*; he published the French version of the sophisticated American magazine *Surfer's Journal*; he wrote essays in which he mused over surfing as 'motion on motion'. Even the way he spoke about the life-cycle of a wave, turning it into a fable about a fatal meeting between two star-crossed lovers, seemed uniquely French.

'The act of surfing ends a long process of creation. Far out to sea, a jet stream in the atmosphere travels up the Atlantic Ocean until the collision between warm and cold air makes a storm. This storm makes a wave, the wave crosses the ocean and comes to the end of the journey. As soon as the wave is breaking she is going to die. It's at this moment when she meets the man. The man is writing his story on her face in these few seconds when the wave is offering her best and perfect shape. It is a good metaphor for how man has built his civilisation and treated nature.'

(I was tempted to remark on the sexual dynamics of his imagery but refrained, unsure to what extent it reflected the gendered nature of the French language. A wave in French is feminine: *une vague*.)

And what of the impact of French civilisation on the South Pacific, I wondered. One French surfer I had met spoke of French Polynesia as being 'empty' and remote from the modern world. It was language eerily reminiscent of the *terra nullius* concept of Australia held by early Europeans. Like the British, the French still regarded the Pacific as something of a colonial playground: the 'ocean of desire' that Bougainville and Cook created with their tales of the South Seas.

Gibus's Pacific was in keeping with this view. 'Tahiti is a kind of surfing dream with glassy waves, tropical landscape, beautiful women and blue lagoons. For Frenchmen, Tahiti is Gauguin and hopefully not any more the nuclear bomb.'

Our final day on the coast dawned sunny and warm with signs of swell and an off-shore wind. As I drove into Biarritz, I could see small, clean waves breaking on the southern beaches. From the narrow lanes of the old town, I found my way along the waterfront path which passed rocky outcrops with little bridges and led finally to La Grande Plage, once known as the *côte des fous* because it was the beach where the mentally ill bathed in the eighteenth and nineteenth centuries. Over-looking this sweeping and seriously powerful surf beach like a colourful stage set loomed a series of deco and art nouveau buildings, a turreted castle, the imposing Casino Municipal and, in the distance, a lighthouse on the rocky headland. The beguiling impression was of surf and sophistication going hand in hand.

The beach was humming with sunbathers, surfers, young families, tanned geriatrics, strutting life guards, beautiful young women and groups of boisterous young men. A third of the population were retirees, and surfing had become central to the local council's push to attract more young people to the town. I hired an unwieldy plastic board from a surfshop opposite the beach and headed for the water. The waves were larger and lumpier than anything I had seen further south. Sudden peaks reared up, peeling quickly then dumping with a hollow thud. There was also plenty of competition as this was the city's main beach. I was just gliding into my first wave, when a young boardrider decided I'd committed a serious infringement and unleashed a howl of outrage. Unless the rules were different here, I was closest to the breaking wave and therefore had right of way. I shrugged it off as the kid's problem and got on with chasing the very fickle and ever-shifting peaks. The heavy hire board was proving hard to manoeuvre but at least I was managing to keep it under control. A little later, a surfer with a manic gleam in his eye, paddled out like a man on a mission and whistled shrilly when I dared to paddle for a wave that he'd earmarked as his. After that, he greedily snatched up every peak that appeared, as if there was no one else in the water. I had been told that French surfers were a mellow bunch, much less aggressive than their Australian counterparts, but there was nothing mellow about the mood here at the *côte des fous*. Later, in one of my surfing guides, I noticed a caveat about Biarritz – 'the stronghold of a fairly possessive local surfing populace'. Indeed. It had been naive of me to expect French surfers to be any more polite, charming or 'civilised' than their counterparts elsewhere.

On the long flight home, I thought once again about my Venice dream and what it had represented to me at the beginning of my surfing odyssey; how enthralled I had been by that wave rising up out of the lagoon. But now I was no longer sure what kind of reconciliation between civilisation and nature I had expected, or even desired.

In the past, on returning from Europe, I had always experienced a period of displacement, of feeling as if I lived at the end of the earth. For a time, the streets would seem too wide and deserted; the pace of life drearily slow; the 'real' world too far away. But this time it was different. This time, when I arrived clutching a toy panda, I did not feel that I was returning to the world's outer edge. Of course, this time, I was glad to be back with my son; he was now my centre. But something crucial had also happened to my sense of the world and of where I belonged.

To go to Europe in search of surf was to see the Old World in a new light. It was, in effect, to relegate Europe to the margins, to put it into perspective. To finally recognise that the centre, if there was one, was not where I had always believed it to be. When I first returned to surfing, I had no idea that my odyssey would become an elliptical journey into the history of the colonisation of the Pacific, an exploration of what the Pacific meant to Europe, and a meditation on the meaning of paradise and asylum. Nor did I imagine how all this might impinge on my understanding of where I lived. But then why bother embarking on any journey if you know exactly where it will lead?

Over the past decade, there had been much debate about the need for Australia to stop seeing itself as a far-flung outpost of Europe. While I could see the economic and geographical sense in the argument, I felt no intimate connection with our part of the world; I had no emotional ties to bring the relationship alive. Surfing had changed all that. Visiting Hawaii and learning about Polynesian civilisation had been the first step. Intellectually I had known that Oceania was where surfing began and that it remained the cynosure of the surfing world, but these facts did not register in a personal way until I looked back on the Pacific from Europe's distance, and was finally freed from Europe's thrall. And now when I thought of the Pacific, I felt strangely possessive. The region in which I lived was defined not by land but by sea – a sea much larger than the Southern Ocean. Perhaps unconsciously I had known that such a mental shift was necessary. Perhaps that was what my Venice dream had been all about. Somewhere between Orwell's nightmarish Oceania and Melville's divine Pacific that 'makes all coasts one bay to it; [that] seems the tide-beating heart of earth', I had found my home.

CHAPTER 8

Slow Boat to Ithaka

SUMMER

Keep Ithaka always in your mind.
Arriving there is what you're destined for.
But don't hurry the journey at all.
Better if it lasts for years,
so you're old by the time you reach the island,
wealthy with all you've gained on the way,
not expecting Ithaka to make you rich.

Constantine Cavafy, 'Ithaka'

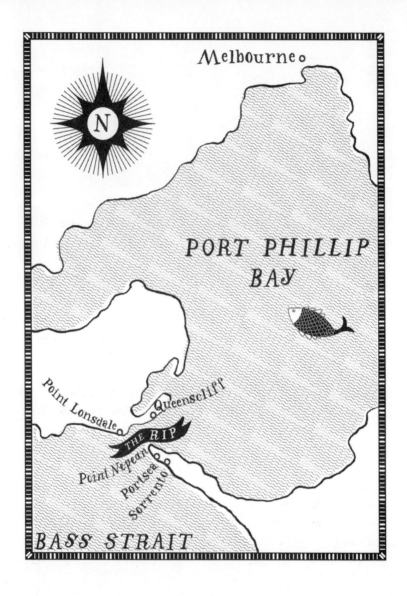

IT WAS A windy, rain-spattered day in early December. We were driving to Sorrento listening to 'Take it Easy' for the umpteenth time, and even *I* was getting sick of it. Our son had discovered that he liked this 'bumpy music' and 'Take it Easy' was all he wanted to hear.

Eventually, I managed to persuade him that there were other tracks worth listening to. 'You'll like this one,' I said, jabbing at the CD player. 'It's called "Take it to the Limit". It's bumpy, too.'

'What's a limit?' came the voice from the back seat.

My partner and I looked at each other and laughed. 'It's what you're always testing us on,' I said.

'What do you mean?'

We tried to explain that a limit was like a rule. In the background, Randy Meisner was crooning, 'Put me on a highway and show me a sign / And take it to the limit, one more time.' The boy was fascinated by signs, especially interdictions at the beach: 'No Camping', 'No Alcohol', 'No Horseriding', 'No Dogs During Daylight Hours', 'No Dumping Rubbish'. As

I read these signs aloud to him (on request), I was reminded how regulated our lives were, and how we became so accustomed to restrictions on our behaviour that we failed to even register them. Curiously enough, these regulations seemed to give the boy satisfaction. There was security in knowing what was allowed and what wasn't; it was one way of learning about how the world worked. At the same time, he was forever pushing the limits we felt obliged to impose upon him. Watching him grapple with these competing impulses – to do as he pleased (satisfy his instincts) and his desire for security – was to observe the origins of a life-long struggle to which there would be no resolution. It was a struggle I understood all too well.

'Take it to the limit, wheee, Take it to the limit, whooo . . .' As the music reached a crescendo, I was scripting the final episode of this book. There would be the triumphant surf at Corsair on those long, hollow waves amid the spectacular scenary of the Heads, and as I drove home afterwards, relieved and exultant, I would be singing 'Take it to the Limit' at the top of my voice, howling with utter abandon like a she-wolf to the moon. I would have pushed myself to my very limits and beyond, I would have confronted my fears and achieved what only two years ago had seemed an impossible and crazy dream. I would have entered that once forbidden zone – a place accessible only to my imagination, a place both close to home and tantalisingly far away – and would have transformed fantasy into fact. I would have realised too – in light of my recent travels and new perspective on the world – that the greatest challenges in life often lay close to home; that you did not have to 'go out far' in order to 'go in deep'. I was on the verge of turning forty and what better way to celebrate?

Yet even as I rehearsed this grand finale, I knew it was too neat, too triumphal, too much the 'perfect' happy ending to ever come true. When I had returned to surfing, I had given myself two years to surf Corsair and that deadline was now past. I was due to hand the manuscript over to my publisher by the end of January. Time had almost run out. When Gally had first expressed doubts about whether I would be capable of surfing Corsair, his reservations had made me all the more determined to succeed. Back then, it had been easy to believe that by the time the deadline loomed, I would be surfing with enough confidence and skill to dispel his doubts. Jack's conviction that I could do it had been crucial, had helped me keep Ithaka in view. For two years, despite the occasional niggling doubt, I had refused to believe that events would not conform to the script in my head. Although I occasionally came across other surfers who raised their eyebrows and muttered darkly about the power of the Corsair wave, I closed my ears. I would pick conditions that were within my ability, even allowing for the difficulties posed by the Rip itself and the hammering nature of the wave.

Now, as January approached, it was becoming apparent that the whole enterprise was much more complicated than I had wanted to believe. For all my research, I had never given proper thought to the logistics of surfing Corsair. Even if a south-easterly was blowing and the surf was small enough, the one-hour lull between the ingoing and outgoing tides might occur too early or too late in the day. On top of all that, there was the dilemma of how to get out there. A boat was the only way – bar walking six kilometres with my board and breaking national park regulations – and a friend of Jack's had promised to take us out from Queenscliff in his couta boat; but his photography business was so demanding that he was finding it hard to spare the time. Soon the schools would break up and holidaymakers would descend on both coasts. As Corsair was the only break in the state that worked on a south-easterly wind, the chances of it becoming suicidally crowded were increasing exponentially.

The beauty of writing fiction is that you have the upper hand over events you invent. There's a glorious self-sufficiency about it, a sense of being a spider spinning a web out of your own guts. You decide what is going to happen and when. You don't have to experience life in all its messiness and unpredictability in order to tell your story. But with non-fiction of the kind I was writing, I was beholden to fickle circumstance – and nothing was as fickle and changeable as the weather in this part of the world. As determined as I was to surf Corsair, I could not will it to happen; not unless I was prepared to be utterly foolhardy and go out in conditions that were beyond my ability.

By Christmas, however, I had established contact with an experienced Peninsula surfer called Drew Smart, who had a boat and was happy to take me to Corsair as soon as the conditions allowed. In the meantime, he was going to Spooks. Would I like to come?

I had heard a lot about Spooks, a break inside the former army territory, on the far side of London Bridge, and had long wanted to surf there. There were stories about a beautiful, half-moon bay with rocky outcrops on each side, and a huge volume of water that pushed into this small area and sucked out in a big, deep rip, with waves breaking on either side of the bay. The right-hander, it was said, was like something you would find in Hawaii.

I met Drew in the carpark at London Bridge. As we shook hands, he flashed a smile that make me think of Mark; he also had the same wavy mop of flaxen hair. I followed him to the end of the public path and over the fence. We scrambled down the cliff to the far end of the London Bridge beach, and then through a small cave, the opening to which was partially closed off with a wire grill that looked like a portcullis – the army's futile attempt to deter surfers from entering. On the other side lay a small rocky beach and, beyond it, the bay of Spooks. I could understand how the game of playing cat and mouse with the army, the sense of entering forbidden territory, would have added to the thrill of coming here to surf. Now that this area was run by the national parks, it was still closed to the public and retained something of that 'off-limits' air. After the long, exposed stretch of Portsea back beach, these small, craggy bays had a secluded, intimate feel.

The late morning sun blazed white-gold on the crumbling cliffs. At Portsea that morning, the surf had looked unpromising, but here there was a regular, neatly peeling, four-foot wave. Surfers were out on both the right-hand and left-hand breaks. Drew suggested we try the left-hander, where only three figures bobbed in the water.

Once I had got my bearings I paddled for a wave, not realising that Drew was further 'inside'. I ought to have pulled out of the wave and left him to it, as surfing etiquette demands, but I wanted him to see me surf so that he might tell me if I was being realistic about surfing Corsair. Our wave yielded a good, long ride – one of the longest rides I'd had – and as a bonus, it reformed closer to shore, hollowing out once again just when it appeared to have run its course.

Once out the back again, I caught Drew's eye. 'Hope you didn't mind sharing,' I said sheepishly.

'Only once.'

There were more waves to be caught. The tide was dropping, exposing the platform of rocks and kelp beneath the water. Drew saw me looking over my shoulder as I paddled for a wave.

'Never look back,' he said. 'Always look ahead to where you're going.' I realised why when the wave I was paddling for sucked back and exposed a pillar of rock. Spooked by this sudden revelation, I moved closer to the channel and tried to slip into the waves further down the line. In time, I told myself, I would learn more about this break, and the way the reef revealed itself at low tide, and I'd become more comfortable with the sight of those rocks. Apart from the pleasure of the waves themselves, there was pleasure of anticipation: the thought of future surfs here, of learning the contours and quirks of this newly discovered place. To think that it had been under my nose for years, while my gaze had been fixed on Corsair. Ithaka was all very well, but here was the Pacific in miniature, well within my grasp.

As we headed back to the carpark, splashing our way across the shallow rock platforms and through the cave again, Drew talked about Corsair. He spoke of the wave there as if it was a living thing that expanded and contracted with every breath. He described how it hollowed out and then fattened up and hollowed again, and how the hollow sections could be savagely steep and how the wave tried to suck you up into its lip and how by the end of the ride your legs would be jelly from the strain of this aquatic tango. He talked also of the dark times there. The time he duck-dived into a shark. The time the engine died and the boat was being dragged towards the crashing waves until some fisherman threw them a rope just before a great wall of water could swamp them.

'Most of the time when you're surfing, you're looking back at land. But out there, you're looking at the side of container ships going past. The topography of the place is like no other. Your only way back is that little boat anchored to that rope, which is taut with the Rip running through it.'

What had I been thinking for the past two years? For all my exploration of Corsair and my attempts to demystify it, for all my conversations with those who had surfed it, I had never really confronted the physical and mental challenges of actually riding a wave there.

I'd surfed at Beacon on 13th Beach – a break that was said to be very similar to Corsair – over a year before, and it had not been an encouraging experience. It had taken me twenty minutes to get through the shorebreak, and once out the back, I understood why it had been such a struggle. The waves were no more powerful than anything I had encountered at Portsea, but they were much faster and more hollow, making a thunderous crack each time they broke. White water around a bombora further out provided a useful indicator of when a set was approaching, but there was no 'safe zone' from which to observe the waves and get their measure without finding yourself in their path. For a time I hovered uneasily, feeling trapped; scrambling to avoid the bigger waves and failing to catch the smaller ones which were breaking further in. Then I asked myself why I had struggled so hard to get out here if I wasn't going to take any risks? When a promising set began to show its teeth, I steeled myself and paddled resolutely for the first wave. The water bulged beneath me and lifted my board, but just when I should have been stroking firmly into the hollowing barrel, I looked down the wave and froze. *Too sheer, too fast.* I wanted out but it was too late. Sucked up by the wave, I couldn't pull back and was forced to take off when the wall was at its steepest, when the lip of the wave was about to pitch. One moment I was on my feet, the next I was in free fall until the wave smacked me down and roared overhead. By now, the worst of it – that moment on the brink peering over the edge – had passed. Although I was still being churned about under water, I felt strangely calm. Within a matter of seconds I'd emerge, bobbing in the wave's wake. Next time, I would know that there was really nothing to fear. The pummelling – if it came to that – was not really *that* bad. The obvious lesson was not to hesitate, not to give way to doubt. But lessons are one thing and life is another. Fifteen minutes later, I did it again. Quailed on the brink and paid the price. 'Look at it like this,' Jack advised me later. 'After wiping out twice like that, nothing should bother you now.' I longed to believe him but doubted it would work like that. Perhaps the truth was that I was out of my league. Perhaps that kind of wave was simply too much for me. *Too sheer, too fast.*

'Tell me honestly,' I said to Drew. 'How experienced do you need to be to surf Corsair?'

He fiddled with his sunglasses, then took them off. 'If we rate waves from one to nine, with one to three being gentler waves like Point Leo, and three to six being the beach breaks like Rye and Portsea, Corsair's up there at nine. That's for degree of difficulty and quality of the wave. I believe you really need to be in that six to nine category – and I put myself at number six – to be a contender.'

So there it was. He was being modest about his own ability but the message was clear. What on earth had made me imagine that I could just roll up in a boat one day and surf one of the most exacting and potentially dangerous breaks in the state?

'I've been kidding myself then, haven't I?'

But something had occurred to him. 'There *were* times when we took the boat out but didn't bother getting in the water because it was only three to four foot. Maybe it's got something to do with respect for the place. We'd only surf it if it was seven foot or more and doing what it does. Anything smaller, and we'd go fishing. So if we were to get you out there when it was three to four foot with a light wind and no one around, it could be possible.'

'You really think so?' I laughed warily. One moment Corsiar was out of the question, the next moment it wasn't. It was hard to know what to think. One thing was clear, though. I was back to waiting, waiting for those elusive wind and wave conditions, waiting for the telephone call, waiting for a moment that *must* eventually happen – but quite possibly not in time for the grand finale I had dreamed of writing.

My son wouldn't remember but I would never forget: the look of terror and delight on his face as he caught his first wave on a boogie board. The breaker came surging across the shallow water, I loosened my grip and let the wave sweep him forward, sending his little body swirling across sand. Furiously blinking the water from his eyes, he staggered to his feet and cried out for more. When not on the board, he loved running out into the waves, shirt-fronting the broken water as it steamed towards him, dashing his body against it. When asked what he liked most about the surf, he would say, 'Bursting the waves!'

Equal to my joy at seeing the boy revel in the surf was the joy of seeing my mother and father return to the water. When my siblings and I were young, our parents would come out with us on their surf mats, and they continued to go out for many years. More recently, though, they had given it away, saying Bass Strait was too cold. But this summer they had bought themselves wetsuits and boogie boards and had rediscovered their old love of the waves. Whenever I arrived at Sorrento and found my septuagenarian father down in the dumps about his health, I would announce that we were all going for a surf. When my parents emerged from the water, the tension was always gone from their faces, their eyes aglow.

A low-pressure system was travelling in from the Great Australian Bight and pushing up the swell. The waves at Porstea were peaking at over six foot. An off-shore wind made for perfect, air-brushed conditions, but the larger sets were virtually unassailable as they rose up and clawed the sky before exploding. The surf was too big for me to even think about paddling out, but it made a glorious spectacle that afternoon as I showed two visitors from Britain, Emma and Peter, over my bit of coast. As we came over the crest of the sandhills and cruised into the Portsea carpark with the ocean fanning out, all wrinkled with swell, I could hardly contain myself. There was a grandeur to the view that no surfer could fail to be impressed by. The stormy sky that had threatened to deluge us that morning had cleared, and Portsea could not have put on a better show.

Peter, a surfing instructor from Devon, took one look and

could not wait to get his board off the roof. 'There's hardly anyone out there,' he marvelled.

Emma, like me, was happy to watch and take photographs. We stood at the water's edge as my son collected seaweed in his bucket. I had first met Emma earlier that year, in the very different surroundings of the wood-panelled, drawing-room interior of a traditional London club near Trafalgar Square. If the setting itself was an unlikely venue for discussing the surf, Emma was an even more unlikely surfer. A successful shoe designer based in London, she escaped from the city whenever she could to go surfing in Cornwall over the summer, and fox-hunting around Dartmoor in winter.

'When you're galloping over the moors, you feel like you're flying. It's the same when you catch a wave – that feeling of getting out of your worldly body, and being in touch with the wild,' she explained in her soft, clipped voice.

The parallels between surfing and riding were not hard to see – the wave as a white horse was a long-standing metaphor in sea literature. However, the idea that surfing might share an affinity with fox-hunting was utterly foreign to me; even disturbing. And yet, as we talked of our shared passion for surfing, I couldn't help wishing that there were more Emmas out in the water. In a world where surfing has become so homogenised, Emma broke the mould of what a surfer is or can be.

I wanted to share my discovery of Spooks with Emma and Peter. When we emerged from the cave, the low slant of the late afternoon sun lit up the great manes of spray blowing back from the solid, eight-foot waves. If Portsea was turning on a good show, Spooks was bringing the house down. When the surf was closing out at Portsea, evidently this was the place to be. Surfers alone and in pairs would suddenly appear over the moonscape cliffs and move with great purpose toward the waves, their faces tense as they scanned the water. All of them were in their thirties or forties, and strongly built.

Each time a surfer took off, he would be consumed by the foaming lip only to emerge into the burnished, unbroken face of the wave to 'take the drop' with heart-stopping aplomb. The waves appeared near-impossible to catch and yet these surfers made it look easy. I could hardly believe this was the same break and the same ocean I had been surfing two days earlier.

Why did I need Corsair when a place like this existed? This was somewhere I could come whenever I wanted; an extension of a beach I knew and loved that was still deeply mysterious to me. No need to pick the lull between the tides, no need to rely on someone with a boat. What had attracted me to Corsair was its symbolism as the Peninsula's farthest extremity, its significance as the 'outer limit' of the coast of my heart. I would never be able to claim it, though, never feel that it was mine. But Spooks was another story. It was a place I could spend the rest of my life discovering, a place I could make my own.

Only now were stories beginning to emerge from survivors of refugee boats that had sunk. They told of the terrible panic, of people screaming and swallowing water, of others holding on to planks of wood or dead bodies floating in life jackets. An Iraqi woman told of the 'doors to hell' opening as she floundered to keep her head above water; of her son saying, 'Goodbye, Mother. Maybe I will see you in paradise,' before he floated away. She told of fighting waves to reach boats in the distance, only to see those boats mysteriously disappear. She clung to a corpse for more than twenty-one hours. Finally, to her great joy, she was reunited with her son. An Iraqi man told of a wave like a mountain hitting their boat and capsizing it. He told of being separated from his wife and their daughter; of swimming towards his daughter as the waves kept tossing her from him until it was 'like when butter melts' and she disappeared. He told of finding her lifeless body floating on the water. These were 'drowning stories' that rivalled those of Homer and Shakespeare, not as literary compositions – although the refugees' eloquence was awesome given the traumatic events they related – but in their intensity and detail, in their power to bring home to us the reality of what it means to fight for your life at sea.

When Odysseus is released from Calypso's thrall, he flees her island on a raft, only to be swamped by a monstrous wave sent by Poseidon. Homer tells how the great wave pins Odysseus under the water, rendering him helpless. When he finally surfaces, he is hit by another wave, which shatters his raft. As he is churned by this 'gigantic billow', Odysseus clings to a single beam of wood 'like a jockey riding'. I liked to think of this moment in *The Odyssey* as the first image of surfing in Western literature; an image that came back to me as I read the stories of the boat people. Here, in the most tragic and bizarre way, the story of surfing and the story of the asylum-seekers intersected. The crude plank on which the first surfer experienced the exhilaration of riding a wave was, at times like this, the same plank to which the shipwrecked seafarer clung. Surfing was not only about paradise found, but about paradise sought and paradise lost.

One morning in mid-January I arrived at work too rushed and preoccupied to think about the weather or the surf. After switching on my computer, I happened to glance out the window and noticed the wind blowing through the leaves of the eucalyptus across the road. Out of curiosity I rang one of the surf report lines that I regularly consulted. As I expected, the wind was on-shore at the beaches on both the Peninsula and the west coast. 'Only for desperados' was the reporter's conclusion. I was about to hang up when the recorded voice added, as if speaking directly to me, that there would be clean three- to four-foot sets at Corsair in the afternoon on the incoming tide. My stomach lurched. *This is it*.

'So we're going for a surf, are we?' Drew laughed when I told him about the report.

Slackwater would happen around five in the afternoon, which gave me plenty of time to get down to Sorrento. I tried to read a book I had to review but couldn't concentrate. For two years I had been working towards this day, although recently I had begun to doubt that it would ever happen. And suddenly, without fanfare, the day had arrived.

The dream of surfing Corsair had enticed me back into the water; had given my journey meaning, tension and a sense of promise. As Constantine Cavafy famously observes in his poem 'Ithaka', the destination had made the journey happen. I was surfing again and would continue to do so for as long as I could. But it was wise to keep in mind the way Cavafy's poem ends: 'Ithaka gave you the marvellous journey. / Without her you wouldn't have set out. / She has nothing left to give you now.'

There were only two letters in the mail box when I went home to collect my board, wetsuit and bathers, one of which was from a bank offering me a life insurance policy. I muttered darkly, screwed it up and threw it in the bin. Then I told myself to get things in proportion. I was just going for a surf.

At the Sorrento boat ramp Drew remarked that the wind was stronger than he would have liked. The sky was darker, too. The boat began to leap over the small chop of the bay. Drew warned me to brace myself for the bumps as we encountered the swell pushing in through the Heads. At Point Nepean we entered the open no-man's-'land' of the Rip. I had been right to think of the Rip as a realm unto itself; neither bay nor strait, its in-betweenness made it all the more difficult to comprehend. A boat full of surfers was anchored and waiting for the change in the tide. Three more surfers were already in the water, one of them being towed into the waves by a jet-ski.

Drew dropped anchor not far from the first boat, putting us side-on to the breaking waves of Corsair. It was some time before I could make sense of what I was seeing, as if I had been suddenly woken from sleep and could not place where I was. On the ocean side of the Peninsula, waves could be seen breaking on the beaches. In the foreground and at right angles to those waves, the swell that had pushed through the Heads was breaking on the sandbank off Point Nepean. From side-on, we could see the waves curling over to form an elliptical hollow, like the eye of a needle, in which the occasional surfer would be crouched.

I talked myself through what I was seeing but something about it refused to register. From this angle, it was impossible to see the take-off point or even fathom where I might position myself to catch the wave. Although I had been here before with John Bryson, his much larger boat had distanced us from what we'd seen, had made it impossible to view Corsair as closely as we were viewing it now. And, of course, I had been in a different frame of mind, still looking at Corsair as a sight-seer, not as someone about to enter the water. I understood now what Drew meant when he spoke about the uncanniness of the place, its utter strangeness. It was a break stripped of all the usual landmarks by which one normally took one's bearings.

The cloud cover was so low it almost looked as if we could reach up and touch it. When the sun occasionally broke through the layers, the sea turned a blinding silver. Most of the time, though, the water was pewter with a greenish patina;

sombre and uninviting. We sat in the boat, exposed to the gusty south-easterly wind, and watched more surfers arrive in boats of various sizes from both sides of the bay. A friend of Drew's anchored nearby, cast a line into the water and attached his fishing rod to the side of the boat; then he jumped over the side and paddled off on his board, with the prospect of something fresh for dinner when he got back. Other surfers appeared on foot from around the fort at Point Nepean, picking their way over the rocks. Meanwhile, in the distance, the great white bulk of the car ferry to Queenscliff slid across the northern horizon like a miniature metropolis traversing the bay.

Low tide was officially at 3.20 p.m. but it took about ninety minutes for the water to stop travelling out of the bay. Then came slackwater, the lull between the tides.

'See how fast they're moving.' Drew pointed to some surfers paddling out to the break from the first boat we'd seen. Once out there, they would have to keep paddling in the direction of the bay to stop themselves from being dragged out through the Heads. Soon, more of their friends were climbing into the water; Drew recognised some of them as sponsored, hot-shot young surfers from the west coast. As the outgoing tide slackened, the waves gained in size and became more shapely. There were now about ten surfers in the water with more approaching, and as we watched, it was becoming clear that these were no ordinary surfers. Even the trickiest waves – those that sucked in their diaphragms and spat out their lips like prima donnas – were being walked all over by these rubber-limbed youths.

'They're good. Very good,' Drew kept saying. Then he remembered the national surfing competition that was supposed to be on at Gunnamatta. But in these conditions, no one would be surfing there.

'Oh great,' I moaned. On the very day that I had finally managed to get here, Corsair was being ripped apart by some of the best junior surfers in the country.

As we watched, a wave lashed out and curled over like a ringmaster's whip. Undaunted, a young surfer slipped through it with gravity-defying ease, all the time anticipating the wave's next move with uncanny precision. In the instant before the wave closed out, he flew like a missile over the back. Drew let out a characteristic cackle. 'And he's just a kid.'

At slackwater, it was time to make a decision. 'Look,' said Drew, pointing to the boats anchored nearby. 'See how their bows are turning. It's like someone has pushed a lever and suddenly there's no tide.'

Before leaving home, I had made a pact with myself that I would go with my gut reaction. If my gut told me the surf was bigger than I could handle, I wouldn't paddle out. But I hadn't anticipated this. The swell wasn't too big but the competition was scorching.

'I thought it would be simple. I thought that once I was here I would know what to do.'

Drew laughed again. 'That's life, isn't it? It's messy. You're never sure if the moment is right. And that's Corsair too. It's elusive. You never know what to expect.'

Leaning against the side of the boat, his arms folded across his chest for warmth, Drew asked me if I'd come out here only because I had committed myself to doing it for this book. And if that was the case, he went on, it was a dangerous thing to be doing, because I was likely to put myself in a situation I couldn't handle, just for the sake of saying I had surfed Corsair. Just for the sake of writing about it.

'Have you noticed,' he added, 'that not a single wave has gone unridden?' Every peak in sight was being snatched up and carved to pieces by these junior pros.

I appreciated Drew's plain speaking and trusted his judgement. He didn't want to push me either way, but if I needed them, he was providing good reasons for me to pull out. There was a succinctness too, a touch of poetry, in the way he summed things up that spoke of his other life as a songwriter.

So this was what it had come to. I'd got this close but had still not quite arrived. 'I guess there's no point, is there?' I said. 'If I've got no hope of getting a wave.' Was I disappointed or relieved? Perhaps both. Next time, though, I would have my bearings, would better understand what I was seeing, would be a little less daunted by the moodiness of the place.

'That's fine by me, either way.' Drew sat down and studied the surf for a while. 'Maybe I'll paddle out for a bit, seeing you'll be here with the boat.' He eased a leg into his wetsuit, then stopped and watched the young hot-shots for a while. There were about twenty surfers out there now. 'Nah,' he said finally, 'it's not worth it.' He yanked his wetsuit off again.

A tanker was approaching from Bass Strait, so we waited to watch it enter the Heads. It swung slowly around and inched silently forward, passing by in the far channel. As we made ready to leave, three teenagers puttered past in an inflatable rubber dinghy. If they had been approaching at the same time as the tanker, they would have been in serious trouble. And they were in trouble enough as things stood: no sooner had they stopped and dropped anchor, than they were bailing water from the bottom of their dinghy. When they were satisfied the boat would remain afloat, the three of them slipped into the water. Such was the lure of this place.

Drew started up the engine and guided his boat as close to the breaking waves as possible for one last look. It was quite a swirling hub of activity, surfers milling and paddling and ducking in and out of the waves.

We doubled back towards the bay, motoring into the wind now, the boat bouncing hard over the chop as we put Corsair behind us. Soon, the inner arms of the bay wrapped around us, drawing us into the gentrified seclusion of the town: the green, well-tended park up on the hill; the little wooden jetties making tentative forays into the water below; the showy houses amid the tea-tree; and, like secular spires, the two limestone towers of the town's surviving hotels. The boat ramp and nearby beach were deserted. It was dinnertime. Turned inwards on itself, the town was oblivious to the pagan gathering, the ritual worship of moon and wave, taking place just beyond its watery outskirts. With the sky turning dusky, it was good to think of surfers out there, their silhouettes making tiny human shapes in the quicksilver limbo of the Rip.

I could feel it waiting for me, biding its time.

Selected Bibliography

Alderson, Wayne, *Surf UK. The definitive guide to surfing in Britain*, Fernhurst Books, West Sussex, 2000.

Anderson, Ross, *Wrecks on the Reef. A guide to the historic shipwrecks at Port Phillip Heads*, Heritage Victoria, Melbourne, 1997.

Bate, Jonathan, *The Song of the Earth*, Picador, London, 2000.

Birtles, Dora, *North-West by North*, as quoted in *The Oxford Book of the Sea*, ed. Jonathan Raban, Oxford University Press, Oxford, 1993.

Bligh, William, *A Voyage to the South Seas*, G. Nicol, London, 1792.

Bognuda, Joan & Moorhead, Leslie, *Gateway to Port Phillip Bay*, Jolbo Studio, Melbourne, 1980.

Breidahl, Harry, *A Guide to Point Nepean's Past*, Conservation & Environment – Victoria, Melbourne, 1992.

Bryson, John, *Backstage at the Revolution*, Penguin, Melbourne, 1988.

—— *Evil Angels*, Viking, Melbourne, 1985.

Byron, George Gordon, 'Childe Harold's Piligrimage,' from Canto IV, clxxxiv. Quoted in *The Oxford Book of the Sea*, ed. Jonathan Raban, Oxford University Press, Oxford, 1993.

Capp, Fiona, *Night Surfing*, Allen & Unwin, Sydney, 1996.

Carey, Gabrielle & Lette, Kathy, *Puberty Blues*, McPhee Gribble, Carlton, 1979.

Carroll, Nick, editor, *The Next Wave. The World of Surfing*, Abbeville Press Publishers, 1991.

Carson, Rachel, *The Sea Around Us*, Oxford University Press, New York, 1989.

Carter, Paul, *The Road to Botany Bay*, Faber & Faber, London, 1987.

Cavafy, Constantine, 'Ithaka' from *The Dark Crystal: An Anthology of Modern Greek Poetry*, selected & translated by Edmund Keely & Philip Sherrard, Denise Harvey & Co., Athens, 1981.

Colum Padraic, *Legends of Hawaii*, Yale University Press, New Haven, 1937.

Cook, James, *A Voyage to the Pacific Ocean*, Nicol & Cadell, London, 1784 (Vol. III by James King).

Daws, Gavin, *Shoal of Time. A History of the Hawaiian Islands*, Macmillan, New York, 1968.

Dening, Greg, *Mr Bligh's Bad Language. Passion, Power and Theatre on* The Bounty, Cambridge University Press, Cambridge, 1993.

Ellis, Rhonda, 'Rainbow Serpents of the Press', Assignment for Journalism II, School Of Humanities, Media & Cultural Studies, Southern Cross University, 2000.

Emerson, Ralph Waldo, 'Terminus', from *The Norton Anthology of Poetry* (Revised), W. W. Norton & Co., New York, 1975.

Faulkner, William, *Thinking of Home, William Faulkner's letters to his mother and father, 1918–1925*, edited by James G. Watson, W. W. Norton & Co., New York, 2000.

Finlay, Jack, *Caught Inside*, Stormy Weather Publications, 1992.

—— 'Wind on the Water', in *Waves of the Sea*, photographs by
   Jon Frank, introduction by Derek Hynd, published by Rip Curl,
   1999.

Finney, Ben & Houston, James D., *Surfing. The Sport of Hawaiian Kings*,
   Charles E. Tuttle Company, Vermont, 1966.

Fowles, John, *The French Lieutenant's Woman*, Panther, St Albans, 1976.

Forbes, David, *Encounters With Paradise. Views of Hawaii and
   Its People 1778–1941*, University of Hawaii Press & Honolulu
   Academy of Arts, Honolulu, 1992.

Freud, Sigmund, *Civilization, Society and Religion, vol. 12*, Penguin,
   London, 1991, especially 'Civilization and Its Discontents'
   & 'The Future of an Illusion'.

Garner, Alice, 'Floating World: Conflicting representations of sea
   and shore in Arcachon and la Teste, 1830–1910'. Thesis (PhD),
   University of Melbourne, Department of History, 2001.

Hamilton-Paterson, James, *Seven-Tenths: The Sea and It's Thresholds*,
   Vintage, London, 1993.

Hawaiian Ethnological Notes, V. 3 ms. HEN., III:108 -118, 'Na Kane
   I hee nalu Oahu'; ms. HEN III:458–462, 'He Nal no Emmalani';
   ms sc. Roberts, Box 2.4, 'O I oe o ka mole uaua o ke alii', translated
   by Mary K. Pukui, Helen Roberts, William Kalaiwaa, Bishop
   Museum Archives, Honolulu.

Hollinshed, Charles, *Lime, Land, Leisure. Peninsula History in the Shire
   of Flinders,* Shire of Flinders, Rosebud, 1982.

Holmes, Tommy, *The Hawaiian Canoe*, Editions Limited, Honolulu, 1993.

Homer, *The Odyssey*, translated by Robert Fritzgerald, Farrar, Straus
   & Giroux, New York, 2000.

Hope, A. D., *Selected Poems*, Angus & Robertson, Sydney, 1975.

Kampion, Drew, *The Book of Waves. Form and Beauty on the Ocean*,
    Santa Barbara, 1989.

Kelly, John, 'Save Our Surf', from *Turning the Tide: Journal
    of Anti-Racist Activism, Research and Education*, Vol. 7, 1994.

Kahanamoku, Duke, with Joe Brennan, *World of Surfing*, Grosset
    & Dunlap, 1968.

Inglis, Andrea, *Victorian Resorts in the Nineteenth Century*,
    The Miegunyah Press, Melbourne, 1999.

Kristeva, Julia, *The Portable Kristeva*, edited Kelly Oliver, Columbia
    University Press, New York, 1997.

London, Jack, *The Cruise of the Snark*, Macmillan, New York, 1977.

Lueras, Leonard, *Surfing. The Ultimate Pleasure*, Emphasis
    International, Honolulu, 1984.

Malouf, David, *Fly Away Peter*, Chatto & Windus, London, 1983.

Massola, Aldo, *Bunjil's Cave. Myths, Legends and Superstitions
    of the Aborigines of South-Eastern Australia*, Lansdowne Press,
    Melbourne, 1968.

Mares, Peter, *Borderline*, UNSW Press, Sydney, 2002.

Martin, Andy, *Walking on Water*, John Murray, London, 1991.

—— 'The History of the Holiday', unpublished version.

McCallum, M. B., 'Surf Time', *Poets At War*, Georgian House,
    Melbourne, 1944.

McDonald, Michael, editor, *The Byron Shire Echo*, 23 October, 2001.
    Article: 'Arakwal Custodian disappointed'.

Michelet, Jules, *La Mer*, Gallimard, Paris, 1983, as cited in *The Basque
    History of the World*, Mark Kurlansky, Vintage, London, 2000.

Moorhouse, Geoffrey, as quoted in *Cricket Quotations: A collection of fine
    paintings and the best cricket quotes.* Exley Publications, UK, 1992.

Morrow Lindbergh, Anne, *Gift from the Sea*, Pantheon, New York, 1983.

Murray-Smith, Stephen, editor, *Bass Strait, Australia's Last Frontier*, ABC Enterprises, 1987.

Nunn, Kem, *The Dogs of Winter*, Picador, Sydney, 1999.

Orwell, George, *Nineteen Eighty-Four*, Penguin, London, 1989.

Paz, Octavio, *My Life with the Wave*, adapted by Catherine Cowan, 1997.

Pollard, Ken, *History of Torquay Surf Life Saving Club*, Torquay Surf Life Saving Club Inc., Torquay, 1996.

Pukui, Mary Kawena & Korn, Alfons, *The Echo of Our Song. Chants & Poems of the Hawaiians*, The University Press of Hawaii, Honolulu.

Raban, Jonathan, *Passage to Juneau. A Sea and Its Meanings*, Picador, London, 2000.

—— *The Oxford Book of the Sea*, Oxford University Press, Oxford, 1993.

—— *Coasting*, Collins Harvill, London, 1986.

Ryan, Maurice, *Time and Tide. A History of Byron Bay*, Northern Star Ltd, Lismore, 1984.

Sharp, Nonie, *Saltwater People. The Waves of Memory*, Allen & Unwin, Sydney, 2002.

Shenk, David, *The Forgetting. Understanding Alzheimer's: The Biography of a Disease*, HarperCollins, 2002.

Slessor, Kenneth, 'Five Bells', *The Collins Book of Australian Poetry*, ed. Rodney Hall, Sydney, 1981.

Smith, Bernard, *Imagining the Pacific – In the Wake of the Cook Voyages*, Melbourne University Press, Parkville, 1992.

Smith, J., *The Cyclopedia of Victoria: An Historical and Commercial Review*, vols 1–3, Melbourne, 1903–5, as cited in *Beside the Seaside*.

South, S. Janet, *George Selth Coppin*, Nepean Historical Society, Sorrento, 1994.

Steinbeck, John, *The Log from the Sea of Cortez*, William Heinemann, London, 1958.

Swinburne, Algernon, 'The Return', *The Oxford Book of the Sea*, ed. Jonathan Raban, Oxford University Press, Oxford, 1993.

Tennyson, Alfred, 'Ulysses', from *The Norton Anthology of Poetry* (Revised), W. W. Norton & Co., New York, 1975.

Warshaw, Matt, Mavericks, *The Story of Big-wave Surfing*, Chronicle Books, San Francisco, 2000.

Wilson, Jack, *Australian Surfing and Surf Life Saving*, Rigby, Sydney, 1979.

Winterson, Jeanette, 'Introduction' to *The Waves*, Virginia Woolf, Vintage, London, 2000.

Winton, Tim, *Land's Edge*, Picador, Sydney, 1993.

Woolf, Virginia, *To the Lighthouse*, Granada, St Albans, 1983.

—— *The Waves*, Vintage, London, 2000.

Wordsworth, William, 'Lines Composed A Few Miles Above Tintern Abbey' from *The Norton Anthology of Poetry* (Revised), W. W. Norton & Co., New York, 1975.

Wright, Judith, *Collected Poems 1942–1970*, Angus & Robertson, 1977.

Young, Nat, with Craig McGregor, *The History of Surfing*, Palm Beach Press, Sydney, 1983.

ACKNOWLEDGEMENTS

More than any other book I have written, this one has benefited from the generosity and help of many people, friends and strangers, who gave their time, their support, their stories and their advice. My thanks go to: Ted Bainbridge, Phillippe Barland, Shay Bintliff, John Bryson, Marcus Burke, Mike Carolin, Geoff Coker, Antony Colas, Greg Dening, Jan Dunton, Mark Dwyer, Rhonda Ellis, Lewis Ferrier, Grayme Galbraith, Alice Garner, Phil Grace, Michael Gordon, Malcolm Hall, Emma Hope, Ivor Indyk, Alan Joyce, Colleen Keane, Rabbit Kekai, John Kelly, Patrick Lataste, Peter Lascelles, Charles Lyne, Russell McConachy, Peter McPhee, Andy Martin, Rusty Miller, Barry Orvis, John Owen, John Sainsbury, Drew Smart, Gibus de Soultrait, Colin Springhall, Glenda Stewart, Phil Trigger, Ronald Ware, Bill Weir, Clare Wright, Val Young, Arnold Zable (for his refugee stories). Thanks to Melinda Capp and Valerie Sutherland for their company on my travels. Thanks to Cheryl Scott and Lori Molent for their part in my earliest surfing adventures. Thanks to Sue Finlay and Carl Finlay for their encouragement. I am deeply grateful to Jack Finlay for his extraordinary support of, and contribution to, this book.

Thanks to Michelle de Kretser for her rigorous editing and to my agent Jenny Darling for her constructive advice. Thanks also to Jacinta di Mase, Sarah Lutyens and Lora Fountain. I am grateful to Rachel Lawson at Allen & Unwin, Ruth Grüner and Verity Prideaux. And once again, thanks to my publisher, Sophie Cunningham, who has been midwife to all my books.

My final thanks go, as always, to Steven Carroll for his professional advice and his support in every way; and to Leo for being such an inspiration.

CREDITS

Excerpts from 'South of My Days', 'Nigger's Leap, New England' and 'Woman to Child' by Judith Wright are reproduced with permission from *A Human Pattern: Selected Poems* (ETT Imprint, Sydney 1996).